100 + Top Tips

for

Understanding Business Finance

Matthew Harris

Published by Ian S Munro

UK Edition

Licence and Copyright Notes

Front and rear cover design - by Deborah Wood.

Printed in the United Kingdom by Printondemand-worldwide.com

A CPI catalogue record for this book is available from the British Library.

ISBN: 978-0-9934658-9-5

The publisher has taken every precaution to ensure that the information contained in this book is accurate and complete.

The legal entity for Ian S Munro is NextSteps Group Ltd, registered office: 2 Crossways Business Centre, Kingswood, Aylesbury, HP18 0RA, UK.

COPYRIGHT OF OTHER AUTHORS:

Books in This Series

BLUE BOOKS FOR PERSONAL DEVELOPMENT

100 + TOP TIPS FOR JOB SEEKERS
ISBN 978-095700-853-3

100 + TOP TIPS FOR DEVELOPING YOUR CAREER
ISBN 978-095700-858-8

100 + TOP TIPS FOR EFFECIVE LEADERSHIP
ISBN 978-0-9934658-6-4

100 + TOP TIPS FOR MANAGING YOUR COACHING NEEDS ISBN 978-0-9934658-7-1

RED BOOKS FOR IMPROVING YOUR ORGANISATION – SMALL AND LARGE

100 + TOP TIPS FOR SETTING UP AND RUNNING AN ONLINE BUSINESS
ISBN 978-099346-580-2

100 + TOP TIPS FOR EFFECTIVE SALES MANAGEMENT ISBN 978-095700-859-5

100 + TOP TIPS FOR EFFECTIVELY USING ONLINE SOCIAL MEDIA
ISBN 978-099346-582-6

100 + TOP TIPS FOR SETTING UP YOUR OWN BUSINESS ISBN 978-099346-585-7

100 + TOP TIPS FOR UNDERSTANDING BUSINESS FINANCE
ISBN 978-0-9934658-9-5

These can all be ordered from www.100toptips.com or from Amazon.

Introduction

This is a finance book for those who really don't think they want to know about finance, but somehow feel they ought to know *something* about finance. Maybe you have a budget for the first time. Perhaps you find yourself with finance responsibilities as a Board Director. You may even appreciate the role that finance plays in almost any organisation and recognise that being able to communicate with your finance colleagues is critical to the success of wherever you work.

Whatever your situation, this book will take you through the basics of business finance and will give you an appreciation for the key terms that you might come across. It won't turn you into a qualified accountant but should allow you to talk to those that are with renewed confidence.

I think of it as learning a foreign language. This book will give you enough to get around and meet your basic needs in a new place (the finance department!). Becoming fluent in finance is possible but will take more time and effort.

Throughout this book we are talking about business finance and not personal finance. All the examples are written from the perspective of running a business, large or small.

There are some areas that are more relevant to large companies, and I have highlighted these. For example, Chapters 9 and 11 are very relevant to a company quoted on the Stock Market (a PLC) and therefore subject to the more stringent regulations mentioned in these chapters. I have included them in this book because there are clear indications that some of these regulations will soon be introduced to non-PLC companies, and they may be things to consider as your business grows.

Contents

Chapter 1

Top 10 Finance Basics

In this chapter:

- A brief history of accounting
- Ledgers and double-entry bookkeeping
- Stakeholders
- Basics of financial statements
- Accruals accounting
- Finance people and systems

1   History of Accounting

- Some form of accounting has probably existed for as long as there has been money. Knowing how much money you have and being able to settle trades must have been an essential part of any monetary system.
- As trading became more sophisticated, it seems likely that accounting followed, and some approaches became standardised.
- It is widely accepted that the first documented system of accounting was recorded by Luca Pacioli, a Venetian mathematician, in 1494.
- Pacioli's work *Summa de arithmetica, geometria proportioni et proportionalita* covers a wide variety of mathematical topics. The one of most interest to us in this book is the section on double-entry bookkeeping – the "Methods of Venice". As James Pickford explains:
  - Double-entry bookkeeping had been in use in Italy for at least a century, but Pacioli is credited with laying down the principles underlying it in the *Summa*, influencing the teaching of finance for generations of accountants up to the modern era [1]
- At the time of its publication, Italy's thriving city states were home to family businesses with international networks of trade, which required increasingly robust methods of management and financial control.

- Pacioli documented the approach used by the merchants to record transactions, and this allowed others to copy the methods, and indeed for them to become standardised. Therefore, accounting is not a new-fangled concept and can clearly trace its documented origins over 500 years. Double-entry bookkeeping remains the foundation of all accounting to this day.
- Incidentally, a copy of Pacioli's original work was put up for sale in 2019. It sold for $1.2m [2]. Which is a lot to account for!

2   Ledgers

- The starting point for recording financial transactions are in the ledgers.
- Ledgers are large books of words and numbers, which maintain the details of every accounting transaction, no matter how small.
- Naturally for most of the history of accounting, these ledgers were maintained by hand, and one can think of whole rooms of accountants laboriously recording entries in large books. These days of course almost all accounting is carried out using computer software, making the process of recording transactions much more efficient, and increasingly automated.
- Nevertheless, the basic ledgers of accounting remain the same, and within any accounting software, the following ledgers will exist:
  - Sales ledger: this records items that have been sold to customers and invoiced to them. It will hold details such as customer name, delivery address, invoice address, contact details, purchase order numbers received, invoices issued to customers, invoices not yet paid by them, and invoices paid by customers.
  - Purchase ledger: this is the opposite to the sales ledger, and records items that have been bought from suppliers. Much of the information is similar with supplier name, supplier address, contact details, purchase order numbers issued, invoices received from suppliers, invoices due to be paid and invoices paid to suppliers.

o **Fixed asset register**: this is a list of all assets held by the company. We will discuss this more in Chapter 3, but examples might be buildings, vehicles, computers, office furniture and so on. It records the initial purchase price of each asset, when it was purchased, the amount of depreciation recorded so far and its current "net book value".

o Cash book: this records all entries of cash in or out of the business. This includes income and expenditure moving through the bank account of the business, and which may be treated as cash.

o **General ledger**: the most significant book of record, the general ledger records all the accounting entries of the business.

  ▪ It takes information from the other ledgers above, as well as entries made directly into the general ledger.

  ▪ The general ledger is made up of a long list of accounts, usually represented by a unique number and which has a description attached to it.

  ▪ Each account is used to summarise the transactions of the business, for future reporting and analysis.

  ▪ As part of any reporting process, a full list will be compiled that summarises all the entries made, and this is called the **trial balance**.

  ▪ The list of accounts is called the **chart of accounts** and getting this list right is an essential part of any accounting system. This is because the financial information that you report on, and therefore use to run your business, can only be as good as the way it is recorded.

  ▪ The chart of accounts will also include **cost centres** which usually represent departments within the business. Each cost centre commonly has a manager who has responsibility for the entries in that cost centre.

- If the chart of accounts is correctly set up to start with, then it makes future analysis significantly easier.
- Even the smallest business can have a chart of accounts than runs to 30 items, and large businesses can have thousands of accounts. Getting the right list and making sure the entries are then recorded in the correct accounts is one of the major responsibilities of business, and accountants work closely with others to ensure that is correct.

3   Double-Entry Bookkeeping

- The core aspect of accounting set out by Pacioli, and which remains at the heart of financial reporting today, is the concept of **double-entry bookkeeping**.
  - o Unless you work as an accountant you don't really need to know the details of double-entry bookkeeping. So, feel free to skip over the next couple of pages. However, you may hear your accounting colleagues talking about debits and credits and setting aside a few pages to cover something so important to them seems worthwhile.
- The essence of double-entry bookkeeping is that any financial transaction requires at least two items to be recorded, and for those two items to be equal and opposite.
- At least one entry is recorded as a **debit** (sometimes abbreviated to DR).
- The opposite entry is recorded as a **credit** (sometimes abbreviated to CR).
- At the very simplest level there will be just one of each entry.
  - o For example, if I sell something for £50 in cash, it requires an entry in the cash book for £50, and an entry in the sales ledger of £50.
  - o As we noted above, these entries will then be recorded in the general ledger as a credit to sales of £50, and a debit to cash of £50.
  - o Debits must equal credits.

- Entries can (and frequently do) get a lot more complicated than that. Even in the above example, if the something sold was a product that the business had purchased (for say £40), and then sold on, the entries would be as follows:

Credit	Sales		£50
Debit	Cost of goods sold	£40	
Debit	Cash	£50	
Credit	Inventory		£40

- In the above example, you will notice that the debits and credits both add up to £90. They are set out in two columns, with debits to the left and credits to the right. This is the traditional way of setting out the general ledger entries and is certainly the way I was taught. It makes it easier to quickly add up the debits and the credits and to therefore ensure that accounts are in balance. The debits equal the credits.
- This is a handy summary of how some of the most common items are recorded. Don't worry about the terminology for now, as we will go through all of these:

Debits	Credits
Cost of goods sold	Sales
Administrative expenses	Interest income
Cash receipts	Cash payments
Fixed asset additions	Bank loan
Depreciation (Income Statement)	Depreciation (Balance Sheet)
Payroll expenses	Liability owed to someone

- One aspect of double-entry bookkeeping that I know causes confusion, certainly for me when I started out, is how this compares to my bank statement.
  - In banking you frequently see reference to amounts being *credited* to your bank account when they have been paid in. Or a positive balance is referred to being in *credit*.
  - Yet, the accounting entries I set out above show cash receipts as being a *debit* not a *credit*.
  - The reason for this is that my bank statement shows the general ledger from the perspective of the *bank*.
  - If I pay money in, then the bank owes me that money, and it becomes a liability for the bank.
  - As my bank balance (hopefully) grows the greater the liability, and therefore the greater the credit.
- It is important to note that just because the debits equal the credits it does not mean that the accounts are correct.
  - It is fairly common for entries to be made into the wrong accounts (mis-postings) particularly if the entries are manual.
  - An important part of any accounting process are the control procedures that are put in place to ensure that the risk of mis-postings is minimised.
- One final word from Pacioli on double-entry bookkeeping. He is famously quoted as saying that "a person should not go to sleep at night until the debits equal the credits". It is that important to get it right!

4   Stakeholders

- Who cares about accounting anyway? I hope that by picking up this book, and making it this far, that you care about finance and accounting.
- It is not just you (and me) though. Whatever your view of accounting and accountants, any organisation is ultimately managed by its finances.
  - I believe this to be the case for government departments, charities, hospitals, schools and so on as well as businesses large and small.

- o Decisions are made based on what can be afforded and the financial impact now and in the future.
- o Those decisions are often assessed subsequently, using financial metrics to figure out if they were successful.
- o Nearly every democratic election has reference to spending plans.
- o If you have a job, you want to get paid.
- o If you have a bank account, you want to know your money is there.
- o And on and on.
- o We rely on accounting in so many aspects of our lives.
- From a business perspective, however, it is possible to distil the list of people who care about the accounts to a relatively short list of stakeholders. This list of stakeholders can vary between businesses, but even then, they will broadly fit into the following categories. These are in no order of importance, and in many ways, they are equally important:

External	External/Internal	Internal
Shareholders	Pension scheme members	Board of Directors
Bondholders	Pension scheme trustees	Management team
Analysts	Parent company	All employees
Banks		
Suppliers		
Customers		
Potential business partners		
Tax authorities		
Regulators		
Industry bodies		
Media		

- o Shareholders: these are individuals or institutions that own a part of the company. This might just be one person for an owner-managed business or could be thousands of separate shareholders for a company listed on a stock exchange. Either way, the financial performance of the business is critical to their understanding of whether the business is successful, and whether their ownership should continue.

- Bondholders: these are individuals or institutions that have loaned money to the company, usually for a fixed period: these are called bonds. Bonds can sometime be traded, just like shares, but unlike shares companies are obliged to pay interest on bonds, and to pay back the original amount on the date it is due.
- Analysts: this is a group of people who analyse company performance and make recommendations as to whether shareholders should buy more (or some) shares, hold on to their shares or sell them.
- Banks: those institutions that provide banking services to your business will always have a close interest in your financial performance. If you borrow money from a bank (and most businesses do at some point in time) they want to be clear that you can repay the amounts out of future profits. Banks will often require frequent updates on the financial performance of the business (monthly or quarterly) as a condition of maintaining a bank account with them.
- Suppliers: those that provide goods and services to your business want to know that you will be able to pay for them. Suppliers often like to have a long-term relationship as well, so look to the financial performance as an indicator that you are a business worth working with in the long-term.
- Customers: similarly, customers are also interested in knowing your business will be there in the long-term. They want to know you will deliver your goods or services on time and to the required quality and want to know you have the financial stability to that. Many products have guarantees in case of breakdown in the future, and customers want to know that you will be there to fix it if necessary.
- Potential business partners: companies are frequently bought and sold or enter into a partnership with another company (for example a joint venture). Whenever these things happen, the financial performance of the business is a critical part of the decision-making process and determines the price at which the transaction takes place.

- Tax authorities: Benjamin Franklin wrote about the only certainties in life being death and taxes. Whilst companies might not be certain to die, they are surely obliged to pay taxes. The details of how companies are taxed outside the scope of this book, but they include corporation tax, stamp duty, national insurance, pay as you earn, value added tax and capital gains tax. Each of these requires accurate accounting to be able to report them to the authorities and failure to do so can have severe consequences. The tax authorities also need to know you can pay the amounts due.
- Regulators/industry bodies: many companies have regulators that take a close interest in the financial performance of their business. These can be sector specific (such as OFWAT for the water industry and OFCOM for telecommunications in the UK) or broader (such as the London Stock Exchange for UK listed companies).
- Industry bodies: many sectors have industry representatives, and they often collate financial information from member organisations as part of their engagement with the wider public.
- Media: business news makes up a core part of many newspapers and news websites, and frequently they refer to financial performance of companies. Most often these are large companies, or those with a large customer base of ordinary households, but any company can find itself covered in the news. I have a personal view that if accounting makes it onto the first page of a newspaper, that is usually not good news.

- o Pensioners/Pension Trustees: pensioners may have two types of interest in your business. If you are a corporation with shareholders, then most pension schemes have investments in shares, and therefore they have a shareholder interest as set out above. In addition, many older companies have pension schemes whereby they promise to pay a pension in the future out of company profits (so-called defined benefit pension schemes). If you have one of these pensions, then you need to know that the financial performance of the company is going to be good enough to pay you upon your retirement. All too often these days companies are struggling to meet these obligations.

- o Parent company: many large businesses operate as groups of companies. These groups have what is known as a parent company, which is at the top of the group structure. Underneath, the companies are known as subsidiaries. Parent companies are interested in the performance of subsidiaries, as they will form part their reported results. Some parent companies get more involved than others in the day to day operations of the subsidiary, which is as much a function of the attitude of the parent company management as anything else.

- o Board of Directors: Chapter 11 talks about governance, but listed companies will have a Board of Directors made up of a majority of non-executive directors. Non-executive directors represent shareholders and other stakeholders and are not involved in the day to day management of the company. However, they are interested in the financial performance of the company and will monitor this and the processes that support the financial reporting.

- o Management team: those managing the day to day activities of the business need to know its financial performance. Are the sales going well, are raw materials being secured at the right prices, are employees being paid on time and so on. Is the business making a profit? Does it have enough cash to meet its liabilities? Are we charging the right prices? These, and many more questions have a financial component, and form a critical part of management decision making.
- o Employees: at the most basic level, employees want to know that the business has enough money to pay them their basic pay. Many employees have some form of bonus plan, often tied to the financial performance of the business, and therefore there is a further interest in how their employer is performing. Beyond that, most people want to work for a growing and successful organisation, that can support the development of their career. Financial performance is one (and I believe the most significant) measure of a successful organisation.

5   The Structure of Financial Statements

- There are three primary financial statements. These are:
  - o The **Income Statement** or profit & loss account
  - o The Statement of Financial Position or **Balance Sheet**
  - o The **Cash Flow Statement**
- These are known as the primary statements as they are required by law and accounting standards to be published but also because by understanding these statements you get a good understanding of the business as a whole.
- Many companies will produce these three statements monthly as part of their management accounts.
- Financial statements will include all the above, but also a comprehensive section of notes to the accounts. The notes summarise the main **accounting policies** and provide explanatory information on significant items.
- We will explore each of these statements in more detail in the chapters to come.
- In addition, there are other statements that are required but which get rather less attention, mainly because they are less easy for non-accountants to understand.

- o Statement of comprehensive income and expense (which can be included with the Income Statement, although is often separate).
- o Statement of changes in equity.
- o Statement of financial position at the beginning of the period where there have been changes in accounting policy made retrospectively, or retrospective restatement of the accounts.

- If you look at a set of published accounts for a listed company, you will often notice that the financial statements don't appear until about halfway through the document. Whilst listed companies have the same obligations regarding accounting, they also have other reporting obligations, and these are usually included in the same document. This is often called the annual report and accounts.
- We won't go into all the details of corporate reporting, but it is required by listing rules to include the following:
  - o A strategic report, which usually includes statements from the Chief Executive Officer and the Chief Financial Officer and sections on the market, corporate strategy and operational performance
  - o A section on principal risks and uncertainties, which often includes a viability statement
  - o A governance section which includes information about the Board of Directors, their backgrounds and responsibilities and the committees of the board (such as audit and risk committee, remuneration committee and nomination committee). I always feel the most widely read pages are those that set out the pay of the senior directors. Employees and the media find this part particularly illuminating!
  - o The report of the external auditors to the shareholders, setting out the work they have performed and their conclusions. When I was an auditor, this used to take up just one page, and was pretty much the same for every company. Modern auditing standards require this to be far more specific to the company concerned and in much more detail. We will discuss the role of the auditor later in this book.

6   **Accounting Standards**

- You will recall that Pacioli codified the principles of accounting 500 or so years ago. However, while the basics were established, there was still plenty of scope for companies to record transactions in any way they wished, which frequently made it difficult to understand a company's performance in comparison with another one, or indeed in comparison with information it had previously reported. The term for this is *creative accounting*, and in this context being creative is not a particularly good thing. Disclosure was also at the discretion of the company management, and there were no set formats for centuries.

- The stock market volatility of the late-1920s and subsequent economic depression started to focus the minds of governments on the need for greater financial transparency for companies, particularly those whose shares were traded on the stock markets. It was believed that at least some of the problems were caused by less than forthright financial reporting practices by some publicly-traded companies [3].

- It was recognised that a set of **accounting standards** would assist in alleviating some of the concerns. These have become known as Generally Accepted Accounting Principles (abbreviated to GAAP) and began to be set out in the US in legislation such as the Securities Act (1933) and Securities Exchange Act (1934).

- Similar observations were being made in the UK, although it was not until the Companies Act of 1948 that these ideas had any legal force [4].

- As commerce became increasingly complex, and interconnected, it was recognised that accounting standards needed to be more rigorously applied, yet more ready to respond to the changing business landscape. Therefore, accounting bodies began to be established to set the frameworks by which companies in that jurisdiction would be expected to abide. These were often nationally based and included the Accounting Principles Board in the US (1959) and Accounting Standards Steering Committee in the UK (1970).

- The increasingly global nature of trade led to the development of common international accounting standards, developed by the International Accounting Standards Board (IASB).

- Whilst some countries may maintain their own standards, today there are two main standard setters:
  - The Financial Accounting Standards Board (FASB) sets US GAAP through Financial Accounting Standards and Accounting Standards Updates. These must be used for reporting in the US.
  - Most other countries make use of International Financial Reporting Standards (IFRS) that have been developed by the IASB.
- There are different levels of standards, which differ mainly in the details around complex transactions and the level of disclosures required. In the UK these are as follows:
  - Listed companies and what are known as public benefit entities (essentially large organisations that provide services to the general public) will prepare accounts to the full IFRS standard.
  - Smaller companies (which include subsidiaries of larger companies) can choose to apply Financial Reporting Standard (FRS) 101 or 102, which have reduced and simplified disclosures.
  - Very small will apply FRS 105 which eliminates a lot of the detail.
  - How company size is determined is set out in the standards based on revenue, assets and number of employees.
  - Charities should use the Statement of Recommended Practice (SORP) which follows the same general accounting rules but has some specific treatments and disclosures.
- It is important to know that there are rules around what can and cannot be done when accounting for a business transaction. You don't need to know the details of all the rules, but you should know a qualified accountant to ask if you think you are doing something new or unusual for your company.

- The accounting rules also change from time to time. Sometimes this is in response to specific emerging issue, and sometimes as part of a longer-term reflection on how standards have been working and their relevance. The two most recent international standards are IFRS15 Revenue from Contracts with Customers and IFRS16 Leases. New standards can take years to develop, and their implementation is often phased in to allow companies to adjust their processes to comply with new requirements. For example, IFRS16 was published in 2016, but only had to be applied after 1 January 2019.

7   Accruals Accounting

- After the double-entry bookkeeping, the next most important accounting concept is that of **accruals accounting**.
- All standard setters have agreed that this is important, and indeed many of the standards over the years have been designed to address the way in which transactions should be accounted for on an accruals accounting basis.
- The essence of accruals accounting is to match income and expenditure in the Income Statement to the period in which it has occurred, which may be different to the period in which it was ordered or paid for. It is commonly agreed that the use of accruals accounting allows the performance of a business to be better reflected in any given period.
- The opposite of accruals accounting is cash accounting. With cash accounting, transactions are recognised only when the cash arrives or leaves the company, regardless of when the actual activity happened. For very small businesses cash accounting may be appropriate but for any business of scale, accruals accounting is mandated by accounting standards.
- I think an example is helpful here:
    - Imagine that today is 15 November and a customer calls you orders £100 of goods from you, that you have in stock and bought for £80. The customer wants them delivered in December, and by agreement will pay for them in January. Your company has a 31 December year end.
    - From a sales perspective, the key question is when should the income be recorded as revenue? November, December or January?

- o In accruals accounting, the answer is December, as that is when the customer has taken delivery of the goods.
- o Similarly, the cost of those goods should be recorded as an expense in December, so that the profit (£20) is recorded in the month that the transaction occurred. This is called an **accrual**.
- o If cash accounting had been used, then there would have been a loss for this year (as the £80 of stock items had already been paid for) and a cash profit of £100 recorded next year. This not only fails to reflect the substance of the transaction (a sale being made in December) but also leads to wild gyrations in the accounts that distort the way business performance is being shown. Big loss followed by big profit.
- o We should (and do) account for the stock items when we acquire them, and for the cash when it is received, but these are recorded in the Balance Sheet and not the Income Statement.
- One common misconception about accruals accounting is that it is used to smooth profits form one year to the next. This should not be the case.
  - o The intent is to match profits and losses to the periods in which the economic activity occurred.
  - o This frequently involves judgements as to when something happened and making and communicating those judgements is very important to the financial statements.
  - o Smoothing profits, however, it is not.

8   When Accounting Goes Wrong

- There are, unfortunately, times when the accounting goes wrong. These are the occasions when it tends to make front-page news, which as I observed earlier is probably not good news.
- There are several high-profile corporate failures that can in whole or in part be linked to failure to apply accounting standards properly. Enron is one example. Of a lesser impact, but still significant, are accounting errors identified by Tesco and BT Italy more recently.

- There are also examples where judgements have been made that have proven to be inappropriate. The collapse of Carillion, for example, is at least in part due to a failure to apply judgements correctly.
- In the immediate aftermath of any significant accounting issue, the company itself and key stakeholders naturally carry out a detailed review of the circumstances. In the most serious of cases regulators will get involved and in the case of Carillion the UK Parliament have interviewed the management and auditors.
- There is inevitably a focus on the adequacy of the accounting standards, the role the management played in applying those standards, and increasingly the role of the auditors in monitoring and reporting on compliance. Apportioning blame can be difficult in complex organisations, although almost inevitably someone loses their job, often the finance chief, regardless of their direct culpability.
- The best outcome is that lessons are learned, both for that organisation and more widely, new standards are developed where necessary and better decision making is made and disclosed.

9   Finance Roles

- Companies are of course free to choose how they wish to organise their finance functions. However, there are some common roles that you are likely to come across in any company large enough to have a dedicated finance team:
  - Chief Financial Officer (CFO) of Group Finance Director: the head of the finance function, with full accountability for the financial results of the company. Also, the Senior Accounting Officer, with a duty to ensure the accounts are an accurate reflection of the performance of the company. CFOs are often seen as the next most senior manager after the CEO, and as such will commonly get involved in a wide range of non-finance activities.
  - Finance Director (FD): you may come across FDs in subsidiaries or business units, where they lead the finance team for that area. In smaller companies the FD will be the most senior finance role (See CFO).
  - Financial Controller (FC): often responsible for the day to day operations of the finance function, including technical judgements on accounting standards. Usually the main point of contact for audit activity. In large companies you may see a Group FC.

- o Finance Business Partner: someone whose role is work closely with a part of the business, often providing support and advice on a wide range of issues with a finance context.
- o Management Accountant: usually the members of the finance team focussed on internal reporting. Sometimes a less experienced member of the team, who might still engage with the wider business but whose primary responsibilities might be processing information and preparing reports.
- o Financial Accountant: usually the person(s) responsible for all aspects of the technical accounting including the preparation of external reports.
- o Accounts assistant: usually the least experienced member of the team, or someone who is focused on a narrow aspect of data entry.
- o Tax manager/accountant: the person responsible for preparing the information that is reported to the tax authorities, and who will also provide advice on the best way to approach certain activities form a tax perspective.

- Many people often see their finance team as being something separate or remote from the rest of the business. Perhaps tucked away in a corner, just adding up numbers and saying "no" to money being spent. I even saw the words 'bean counters' being used recently to describe the CFO and their finance team.

- Whilst this may have been true in the past, I truly believe that a modern finance function is forward thinking and supportive of business growth. They do still have responsibilities for the stewardship of the finance for the organisation, but modern finance professionals understand that without sustained growth, there is unlikely to be an organisation to support. This involves having a much closer working relationship between all parts of the business and making sure that the finance team are truly engaged with business and supporting the operational teams. Deloitte have written extensively on this, and have carried out research, based around their Four Faces of the CFO model [5]. I see this book as being part of making that connection.

- There are many types of qualified accountants. Several national organisations exist to regulate the profession and to set standards. In most cases, the requirements to qualify are the same, and include a series of examinations combined with a minimum of up to 3 years of practical experience. Once qualified, accountants are required to maintain their knowledge through continuing professional development (CPD) such as training courses.
- I have worked with a range of accountants with different qualifications. It really does not matter to me which qualification an accountant has, so long as they demonstrate the attitude and aptitude to be effective. However, you may be in the position of hiring an accountant, and therefore would find it helpful for the myriad of qualifications to be demystified. In the interests of full disclosure, I am a member of the ICAEW:
    - ACCA – Association of Chartered Certified Accountants. A UK-based organisation, with a broad focus on both technical accounting and broader financial management. Qualified members use the letters ACCA or FCCA after their name.
    - CIMA – Chartered Institute of Management Accountants. A UK-based organisation, with a bias towards management accounting and financial management, and less emphasis on some of the more technical aspects of finance. Qualified members use the letters ACMA or FCMA after their name. They may in addition use CGMA.
    - ICAEW – Institute of Chartered Accountants in England and Wales. A UK-based organisation, with a bias towards technical accounting and auditing. Qualified members use the letters ACA or FCA after their name.
    - ICAS – Institute of Chartered Accountants of Scotland. A UK-based organisation, with a bias towards technical accounting and auditing. Qualified members use the letters CA after their name.
    - CIPFA – The Chartered Institute of Public Finance and Accountancy. A UK-based organisation that is aimed at those who work or want to work in the public sector. Many of the topics covered are as for the other institutes, but there is bias towards government accounting.

- o CPA – Certified Public Accountant. The US equivalent qualification largely focussed on technical accounting and auditing. Qualified members use the designation CPA.
- Other countries have their own accounting qualifications, with broadly equivalent requirements.
- It is also not uncommon for senior members of the finance team to have an MBA in addition to, or instead, of an accounting qualification.
- It is a valid question to ask why there are so many different bodies, and could they not be consolidated? There is a lot of history, and although there have been attempts to merge some of them over the years, these have all failed. The existing members usually favour their institute over any other, even if this is to the detriment of making things simpler for the rest of the business world.

10   Finance Systems

- Even the smallest businesses will make use of finance systems. With the ready availability of cloud solutions, the cost of having a finance system is much lower than it used to be.
- For smaller businesses, there are several accounts systems that offer the basic transaction processing and reporting that is required. Common ones are Quickbooks, Sage, Wave and Xero.
- Larger businesses need more sophisticated systems, which often need to operate in multiple sites, across many different countries. It is common to integrate several business processes into one system, and this is often known as an Enterprise Resource Planning (ERP) system. It will carry out all the basic accounting and reporting, but will often include sales, production, distribution, customer relations management (CRM) and payroll activities. Again, many different software companies provide solutions, common ones being Oracle, Sage, SAP and Workday.
- I have also seen instances where other finance systems are used to support more technical aspects (such as tax, consolidation or complex reporting) in addition to the main accounting system.
- The other most common tool, in my experience, is the spreadsheet (usually Microsoft Excel, although occasionally Google Sheets; I am showing my age when I mention I learned using Lotus 123!). Despite plenty of evidence of spreadsheets being prone to containing mistakes [6], sometimes major ones [7], it has still been the reporting tool of choice in my career.

- Whilst you might not need to know the detail of how your company's finance system works, you may find yourself needing to at least understand what system is used and how effective the finance team and others find it in practice.

YOUR NOTES FROM CHAPTER 1

Chapter 2

Top 10 Tips for the Income Statement

In this chapter:

- What is an Income Statement?
- The layout of the Income Statement
- Key headings and what they contain
- Depreciation and amortisation

The financial statement that typically gets the most focus in any business context is the Income Statement, which is also known as the Profit & Loss Account (or P&L). We will look at what this statement is for, how it is prepared and what you might look for when you see one.

1   Income Statement

- The Income Statement is for tracking performance at its simplest level: have the sales that we have achieved generated more income than the costs we have incurred?
- Another way of looking at it is what has the yield been for the effort that has been put into the business?
- A good friend of mine talks about this in terms of an apple tree. How many apples have been produced? Is this a good or bad number of apples relative to previous years, and expectations?
- The Income Statement only looks at performance over a short period of time. For external stakeholders this will be for a 3-, 6- or 12-month time period. For those in the business a monthly Income Statement is the norm and allows a ready track of performance as the business is operating (see also Chapter 6).

- Using the apple tree analogy, fruit is only produced once a year, and the performance of one year does not necessarily mean the next year will be the same. It could be better or better, or worse depending upon the prevailing conditions and how the tree has been treated in the year.
- The Income Statement is usually straightforward to produce, and a minimum expectation of your finance team or accountant is a monthly statement of performance produced reasonably quickly and accurately so that decisions can be based on the latest information.

2   Layout of the Income Statement

- The layout of the Income Statement is determined by accounting standards and company law. There are some, minor, variations in format, but the following is typical. The grey shaded rows are sub-total lines:

Income Statement Heading	Notes
Revenue	Also known as Sales or Turnover or Income
Cost of Sales	
Gross Profit	Sub-total: Revenue – Cost of Sales
Operating Expenses	Often abbreviated to Opex
Operating Profit	Sub-total: Gross Profit – Operating Expenses
Non-Operating Income/Expense	
Earnings Before Interest and Tax	Also known as EBIT Sub-total: Operating profit +/- Non-Operating Income/Expense
Interest Income/Expense	
Earnings Before Tax	Sub-total: Gross Profit – Operating Expenses
Tax	
Earnings After Tax	Also known as net profit. Total: Earnings Before Tax +/- Tax

- Typically, there will be several columns for the Income Statement information. One will be the actual period being reported on, but there will be a few comparative periods of data as well. These may include:
    - The equivalent period for the last year.
    - The previous month or year.
    - Budget or forecast (see also Chapter 7).
- All companies break down each of the main headings into more detail. This is primarily to allow more analysis to be performed either for internal management information, or for external reporting to specific stakeholders (for example tax authorities need specific detail on certain Income Statement categories as part of their returns). The larger and more complex the organisation the more detailed the accounts will be; there can easily be 10,000 accounts for large companies.

3   Revenue

- Revenue is the income earned by the business in the period. It also known as sales, turnover, income or the top line.
- It reflects the activity of the business in delivering goods or services to customers.
- It is a headline number frequently quoted in any review of a company's results and quickly becomes a shorthand for whether the company is being successful or not.
- One of the critical points to note is that is does necessarily equal what those customers have actually paid for, or indeed necessarily what they have been billed for. This is one of the most important aspects of accruals accounting, called **revenue recognition**.
- We discussed an example for goods earlier on, but things can get a lot more complex than the simple illustration used then. So much so, that there is a specific accounting standard on the topic: IFRS15 Revenue from Contracts with Customers.
- The principle is that revenue should be recognised when the goods are transferred from the seller to the buyer, or the services are delivered to the buyer.

- For goods, there can be complicating factors where the items are shipped over time, where there is a right to return the goods, or where ownership of the goods only transfers at a later point.
- For services, the exact delivery of complex or long-term contracts can give rise to the need to make difficult judgements on the outcomes of those contracts. One recent example of this not going well was Carillion, where a series of judgments proved to be optimistic, and led to the downfall of the company.
- We do not have the scope here to consider every variation of revenue recognition, but you should ask your finance colleagues:
  - What is our revenue recognition policy?
  - What information do you use to support our revenue recognition?
  - How reliable has that information been in the past?
  - How do we disclose the judgements we are making internally and externally?
  - What more information would be useful to understand our revenue recognition?
- One other thing to note is that in Europe at least, the revenue is always quoted excluding sales tax (Value Added Tax or VAT). Customers may be invoiced including VAT but the company is only collecting the tax on behalf the government, and must pay the money over soon afterwards. Therefore, this is not an income to the company and so is disregarded.

4   Cost of Sales

- These are the direct costs of delivering the revenue identified above.
- These will include some of the following:
  - Raw materials used in manufacturing.
  - The direct costs of manufacturing including electricity, energy, labour costs, factory operating costs and so on.
  - Factory rent.
  - The cost of goods purchased for resale.
  - The costs of people delivering the services.
  - Depreciation of factory equipment.
- As with revenue recognition, there may need to be a judgement about what costs are directly applicable to the revenue generated, and the timing of these costs.

- Here the most important concept is matching. Revenue and costs should be matched to show a true gross profit.
- **Gross profit** is then a sub-total that shows how much profit the business has made directly from its operating activities. Bear in mind that there are other costs associated with running a business (which we will come to) and so if costs exceed revenue at this point (a gross loss) performance of the business is very poor and likely not sustainable.
- As with revenue, VAT is usually disregarded as it can be recovered from the government as part of the VAT process. The exception to this is where a company makes supplies that are exempt from VAT and where recovery is restricted.

5   Operating Expenses

- These are the all the other expenses, except interest and tax, that are incurred in running the business. Often these **operating expenses** are known as overheads and may also be abbreviated to **Opex**.
- Examples include:
    - The salaries of the management team.
    - Depreciation of office equipment.
    - Marketing and advertising costs.
    - Office rent.
    - Office expenses such as energy, telephones and internet access, and business rates.
    - Other administration costs, including those of the finance team!
    - Insurance costs.
- As with all the other items on the Income Statement, care needs to be taken in how the costs are recognised, to ensure that they are matched to the relevant period.
- Deducting these from gross profit gives a sub-total for **Operating Profit.**
- Whilst not desirable, it is at this level that you may see losses being recorded. If a company has had a bad year or has overheads that are too large for its operations, then losses may be made.

- Losses are not necessarily terminal for company, although sustained losses are likely to be without a substantial change in the business and funding arrangements.

6   Non-Operating Income / Expense

- These are items of income and expense that are not a core part of the business activity, but nonetheless generate a profit or loss that needs to be included.
- For example, if you sell a tangible fixed asset and make a gain (profit) or loss on disposal (see the chapter on the Balance Sheet).
- For example, if you have an office building, but have some spare rooms and therefore sublet a portion of it. The rental income is not a core part of your activity and so would be recorded here.
- Another example are the company's share of the results of joint venture and associate companies, and Costain Group record these as non-operating income in their accounts.
- Adding or deducting these from operating profit gives **Earnings Before Interest and Tax** (or '**EBIT**') also known as Profit Before Interest and Tax (or 'PBIT').
- EBIT is another commonly quoted figure and news articles will frequently mention profits, by which they generally mean EBIT.

7   Interest Income / Expense

- Where company borrows money from a bank or other lenders (see also Chapter 10) the lender will charge the company interest. The cost of this financing will be shown in this line of the accounts.
- If the company has surplus cash, and has managed to generate some interest income, then that too will be recorded in this area, albeit on a separate line.
- The purpose of separately showing interest expense from the other expenses is so that lenders can easily see the financing costs that the company is incurring, and that will help inform future lending decisions.
- At the risk of repeating myself, interest should be recorded on an accruals basis, to show the interest due in the period which is often different to what was actually paid.

- The next sub-total is **Earnings Before Tax** (or '**EBT**') also known as Profit Before Tax (or 'PBT').

8   Tax

- The penultimate line of the Income Statement shows the cost of business (or corporation) tax. Specifically, this is the tax due on the profits of the company. It does not include any sales or value added tax, nor other taxes that the company might have to pay such as payroll or property taxes.
- Company taxation is extremely complex, and varies significantly from country to country, and indeed within countries in many cases. We do not have time to explore the detail of tax here, beyond saying that it needs to be accounted for based on a detailed calculation of what is due to the tax authorities for the period concerned.
- Usually the tax will be paid sometime after the period end, sometimes several years after where the tax treatment of an item is deferred.

9   Depreciation and Amortisation

- It is worth taking a brief detour into depreciation and amortisation, what they are and their impact on all three primary financial statements.
- Depreciation is a recognition that sometime a company buys something that has a long-term use within the business. By long term-term we typically mean more than 12 months. These are called **non-current assets**, and we will discuss them again in the next chapter.
- There are two main types of non-current assets:
  - Fixed assets such as land, buildings, trucks, cars, computer equipment, robots, office furniture and so on. This is by far the most common type of long-term asset, and nearly every company will have some of these.
  - Intangible assets, which arise usually when another company has been acquired (merger or acquisition). These are rarer, albeit not uncommon, particularly in larger businesses. They include the value of an acquired brand and list of customers (known as goodwill).

- Accounting standards require that recognition is made that using these assets in the business has some cost associated with them. This will not be the full cost of the asset in the first year (its acquisition cost), as we need to match the costs over the time that asset will be used in the business. This time is called the **useful economic life** of the asset. At the end of its useful economic life it might still be worth something, which is known as the **residual value**. The difference between the acquisition cost and residual value is spread over the useful economic life and is called **depreciation** of fixed assets or **amortisation** of intangible assets.
- An easy comparison to personal finances is buying a car. Let's say you decide to buy a car for £30,000, will aim to keep it for 4 years, and then hope to get £10,000 from selling it before buying another one. Here you can see that:
    - The acquisition cost is £30,000.
    - The residual value is £10,000.
    - The useful economic life is 4 years.
    - Depreciation expense of £20,000 must be spread over 4 years.
- There are a few different ways of spreading the depreciation expense, but by far the most common method in my experience is the straight-line method. This is a simple formula as follows:

$$\text{Annual depreciation expense} = \frac{\text{Acquisition cost} - \text{Residual Value}}{\text{Useful Economic Life (years)}}$$

- In our example the depreciation will be £5,000 per annum (or £416.66 per month).
- The **net book value** (or '**NBV**') of an asset can be determined at any one time by taking the acquisition cost and deducting the total depreciation charged to date. In our example, the net book value of our car after a year is £25,000.

- There are judgements being made here, of course. How does a company know what the residual value will be? How can they be sure the asset will last as long as they have said? Will it last longer, or less time? Even the acquisition cost can have some interpretation, perhaps where the installation has been part of a wider piece of work that might otherwise be expensed. Accounting standards recognise this, and some adjustments can be made as new information becomes available. Normally this will be to increase the expense, not reduce it, and adjustments to previous accounting periods are generally not permitted for external accounts.
- Most companies classify their assets into broad categories (for example, buildings, vehicles, computer equipment, machinery) and will depreciate all the assets in that category in the same way. It is common for computer equipment to have a much shorter life than an office building for example, which reflects how quickly computer equipment needs to be replaced.
- There are some common exceptions to the general rule of depreciation:
  - Land that is owned by the business is generally considered to have an infinite life and therefore no depreciation is charged for land.
  - If you become aware that an asset has deteriorated significantly, and is no longer worth its current net book value, then you must increase the depreciation cost to date immediately to recognise its true current value.
  - Sometime assets go up in value (particularly buildings) but in general you are NOT allowed to reverse depreciation already incurred or increase the value. There are exceptions to this exception, but they are not common.
- We will look at this again the Balance Sheet and Cash Flow Statement.

10   EBITDA

- The reason for taking a diversion there, is because there is another Income Statement sub-total, that usually does not feature on the statement itself, but is often used in businesses.
- This is called **Earnings Before Interest, Tax, Depreciation and Amortisation**, or **EBITDA**.
- This sub-total can be calculated by taking the EBIT sub-total and then adding back any depreciation and amortisation expense. It shows the profit before any accounting adjustments relating to the acquisition of long-term assets, which may have happened some time ago, and therefore be out of the control of the current organisation.
- It is a measure often used by external analysts of company performance, and therefore is sometimes used by companies for internal reporting as well.

YOUR NOTES FROM CHAPTER 2

Chapter 3

Top 10 Tips for the Balance Sheet

In this chapter:

- What is a Balance Sheet?
- The layout of the Balance Sheet
- Key headings and what they contain

The second most prominent financial statement is the Balance Sheet. We will look in this chapter at why it is important, the principal categories of any Balance Sheet and some of the things you might look for.

1   Balance Sheet

- The Balance Sheet is a statement of the financial position of the business at a point in time and indeed is formally called the Statement of Financial Position in accounting standards.
- It is often referred to as a snapshot of the business, as it is only looking at a specific point in time.
- Using the apple tree analogy from the previous chapter, the Balance Sheet is like the trunk of the tree. It shows the fundamental strength of the tree today, and over time you would expect to see it grow. Whilst minor damage will not have an impact on the yield, any significant damage or disease can dramatically reduce the fruit crop (or profit outcome) or indeed kill the tree (or company).
- The Balance Sheet lists all the assets and liabilities of the business at a date.

- Assets are always listed first, and are items held for use in the business. Liabilities are obligations that the business must pay someone, and these are listed second. We will look at the details of these in this chapter.
- The Balance Sheet is usually straightforward to produce and is typically prepared in parallel with the Income Statement; it should be available with the same frequency from your finance team.

2   A Question of Balance

- In a Balance Sheet, the assets must equal the liabilities. It must balance:

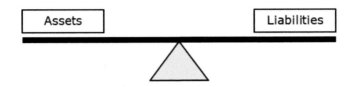

- The fundamentals behind this logic are that for the company to acquire assets, it must generate the same level of funds to pay for these assets, and these are liabilities.
- There are, however, some ratios that we will look at later in this book, that take the Balance Sheet assets, and compare these with some of liabilities to show the overall strength of the business (see Chapter 8).

3   Layout of the Balance Sheet

- As with the Income Statement (and the Cash Flow Statement that we will look at in the next chapter) there is a prescribed layout:

Balance Sheet Heading	Notes
Non-Current Assets	*Also known as Long-Term Assets*
Current Assets	*Also known as Short-Term Assets*
Total Assets	*Sub-total: Non-Current Assets + Current Assets*
Current Liabilities	*Also known as Short-Term Liabilities*
Non-Current Liabilities	*Also known as Long-Term Liabilities*
Total Liabilities	*Sub-total: Non-Current Liabilities + Current Liabilities*
Net Assets	*Total Assets – Total Liabilities*
Equity	*Also known as Capital & Reserves*
Total Equity	*Total Equity MUST EQUAL Net Assets*

- You may sometimes see the Balance Sheet presented slightly differently, with the same headings but just reordered slightly as follows:

Balance Sheet Heading	Notes
Non-Current Assets	Also known as Long-Term Assets
Current Assets	Also known as Short-Term Assets
Total Assets	Sub-total: Non-Current Assets + Current Assets
Equity	Also known as Capital & Reserves
Non-Current Liabilities	Also known as Long-Term Liabilities
Current Liabilities	Also known as Short-Term Liabilities
Total Liabilities	Sub-total: Non-Current Liabilities + Current Liabilities
Total Equity and Liabilities	Total Equity and Liabilities MUST EQUAL Total Assets

- Either presentation is fine, provided all the headings are present and correct.
- As with the Income Statement there are typically multiple columns of data, with comparative periods. Often the comparative will be the previous year end point, as that is latest published snapshot of the business. In that sense it might be different to the Income Statement, where the same time last year is often used.
- Furthermore, in my experience a detailed month to month budget or forecast for the Balance Sheet is less common. Therefore, this will not always be one of the comparison data sets.

4   Non-Current Assets: Intangible Assets

- The first category of non-current assets is called **intangible assets**.
- They are a type of asset that has no physical form, and includes things like goodwill, patents, trademarks and software.
- Not every company will have these, and because they have no physical form the accounting rules are strict on what may be included and how it is accounted for.
- The most common type is *goodwill*. Goodwill is the difference between the value of the assets and liabilities of a company and its overall worth. This difference arises because the company has a strong reputation, brand awareness, unique product, customer loyalty, locations and so on. For example, the worth of Coca Cola as a company far exceeds the value of its production plants, offices and so on. The secret recipe, brand awareness and availability around the world have significant value.
- It is very difficult to put a price on goodwill, and therefore accounting standards do not permit you to create your own valuation and record that as an asset.
- However, goodwill does commonly arise when one company buys another. For example, Company A might buy Company B for £100m. However, the net assets of Company B might be £80m. Company A has decided that the brand value, customer lists and other aspects have a value of £20m, and this is the goodwill value. Company can record the £20m as goodwill in its Balance Sheet.
- Accounting standards require all intangible assets to be subject to an **impairment test** at least annually. This is a test to decide if the value of the intangible asset has gone down. How this is determined is complex, and beyond the scope of this book, but just know that it happens, and your finance team will lead the calculation. If the value of the intangible has gone down, then the value on the Balance Sheet will be reduced and the cost will be shown in the Income Statement as **amortisation**.

5   **Non-Current Assets: Fixed Assets**

- **Fixed assets** are physical assets that exist and can readily be seen. These are far more common than intangible assets, and almost any company will have some of these.
- They are assets owned and used in the business such as offices, factories, production equipment, vehicles, computers and so on.
- They are often known as *Property, Plant and Equipment* as that describes the type of assets in this category.
- They are long-term assets as they are usually held for more than one year. They are not held to sell in the short-term, but instead are expected to be used to generate income in the long-term.
- Acquiring these types of assets is often known as **Capital Expenditure** (or **capex**) as distinct from opex that we looked at in the Income Statement.
- The assets are shown on the Balance Sheet at what is called their *Net Book Value*. **Net Book Value** (or '**NBV**') is the difference between the cost of the asset when it was acquired, and all the depreciation associated with that asset since then. You will recall from the previous chapter that depreciation occurs as an asset is used within the business. We used the example of a car. Each year the depreciation is charged as a cost to the Income Statement. The balancing entry to that is in the Balance Sheet.
- Revisiting our car example, we decided to buy a car for £30,000, aiming to keep it for 4 years, and then hope to get £10,000 from selling it before buying another one. We saw see that:
  - o   The acquisition cost was £30,000
  - o   The residual value was £10,000
  - o   The useful economic life was 4 years
  - o   Depreciation expense of £20,000 had to be spread over 4 years
- The NBV is follows:

Period	Acquisition Cost	Annual Depreciation	Accumulated Depreciation	NBV
Year 0	30,000	0	0	30,000
Year 1	30,000	5,000	5,000	25,000
Year 2	30,000	5,000	10,000	20,000
Year 3	30,000	5,000	15,000	15,000
Year 4	30,000	5,000	20,000	10,000

- The annual depreciation will be shown in the Income Statement (£5,000 in each year) and the NBV is what will be shown in the Balance Sheet.
- Different assets will have different depreciation rates attached to them, to reflect the different lengths of time they might be expected to last. Companies can determine their own useful economic lives, although they must be reasonable. Typical examples I have seen are:
  - Buildings: 20 – 50 years
  - Factory Equipment: 10 – 30 years
  - Other Equipment: 3 – 10 years
  - Vehicles: 3- 10 years
  - Computers: 2 – 5 years
- You can imagine that a very large business will have thousands, or indeed millions, of fixed assets. Therefore, the Fixed Asset Register becomes an important part of the accounting system. It records all the assets of the business, often with a unique serial number, their location and the initial cost and all the subsequent depreciation.
- Fixed assets usually have a very significant value attached to them (millions of pounds in the case of land or buildings) and therefore it is common for an exercise to be carried out that confirms that the assets still exist (things like computers can often be misplaced or stolen) that it is in good condition and still working. Many companies do this annually and is an exercise you might be asked to assist with.
- The condition of the asset is important. Whilst you may set out an annual depreciation cost of an item, if it deteriorates more quickly, then more depreciation must be recognised. For example, take our car above. If we look at it and the end of year 3, and now realise that it has done a lot more miles than we expected, has a lot of scuffs and other damage, we may now think that it is not worth £15,000, but only £8,000. We would therefore depreciate it not by £5,000 in year 3, but by £12,000 to recognise its reduced worth. We would also have to assess what it might be worth in 12 months' time in order to get the correct depreciation charge for year 4.
- Accounting rules only allow you to accelerate depreciation not reverse it. So, if you think the car is worth more at the end of the year, that is tough.

- The exception to this is when you sell a tangible asset. At the point of sale, you will remove the acquisition cost and the accumulated depreciation for that asset from the fixed asset register and the Balance Sheet. The difference between what you received for the asset and its NBV will be a gain or a loss on disposal and will be shown in the Income Statement as non-operating income or expense (see Chapter 2).
- There are two other exceptions of note:
  - Land will be included as a tangible fixed asset at its acquisition cost. However, as we discussed in the last chapter, it is generally assumed that land has an infinite life and therefore will not have an annual depreciation charge. If there is some evidence that the land value has been reduced, then depreciation would be appropriate, but that is the exception to the exception. Usually there is no depreciation on land!
  - Due to the enormous number of potential fixed assets in large companies, it is common for a company to decide not to include small value items as fixed assets. Each company will make its own decision, but often it can be up to £5,000 (or even more) which means common items such as computers and printers may not be capitalised (included as fixed assets). These assets will simply be included as a cost in the Income Statement, usually as operating expenses. There is no depreciation and they are not included as fixed assets.

6   Current Assets

- **Current assets** are much more straightforward. These are items held in the business where the objective is to turn them into cash as soon as possible as part of the normal business cycle. The assets that are hardest to turn into cash (least liquid) are listed first, and the easier ones (including cash) are listed last.

- The least liquid of the current assets are stocks of goods, also known as **Inventory.** There are three types of inventory:
  - o Raw materials or components. These are items that have not yet been assembled into a finished product. These may be slow to turn into cash because you must put them through the factory, make the product, deliver the product, send an invoice and then collect the cash.
  - o Finished goods. These are the completed products that are ready to ship to the customer. It may still take time to turn them into cash as you must deliver the goods, send an invoice and collect the cash.
  - o Work in progress (also known as WIP). This is where a product might take some time to complete, and the business is part way through assembly. Therefore, it is neither raw materials nor finished goods but is in a stage somewhere in between. Since the Balance Sheet is a snapshot, it is important to understand what has been completed. WIP also applies to service companies where they might deliver a service over time, but not complete it or invoice it until the end.
- The next current asset is called **Receivables** or **Debtors**. This is where a customer has received goods or services but not yet paid for them.
  - o In business it is very common have a gap between invoice and payment. 30 days is not unusual.
  - o You do want this period to be as short as possible though, as you have paid to assemble and deliver the goods, and you want the customer to pay you as soon as possible.
  - o Sometimes customers will be slow to pay, either deliberately to hold on to cash, or because they cannot afford to pay. It is therefore essential to maintain good relationships with customers, keeping in regular contact with them to understand any issues they may have with the products or services they have received, and to check that they will be paying on time.
  - o Large companies often have **Credit Control** departments to lead this activity.

- **Prepayments** are the next category of current assets. These are often included as part of Receivables.
  - o Prepayments occur when you pay for something in advance of it being delivered. It is an asset because you have the future right to a service that you have paid for, and in theory you could cancel and get a refund.
  - o A common example here is an insurance premium: these are usually paid annually in advance and therefore would be recognised initially as fully prepaid.
  - o Over time the service is used up; each month $1/12^{th}$ of the cost would be charged to the Income Statement, and the Balance Sheet prepayment would be reduced accordingly so that after 12 months the prepayment would be nil.
  - o This is a great example of how cash accounting differs from accruals accounting: the cash has been paid out, but the Income Statement effect is delayed.
- The final, and easiest, category of current asset to understand is **cash** held in the bank (or even as actual cash on the premises). This is money readily available to be used by the business and can typically be accessed in a very short time.

7   Non-Current Liabilities

- **Non-current liabilities** (also known as Long-Term Liabilities) are obligations that the company has, but which do not fall due for at least a year form the Balance Sheet date.
- These might include long-term loans made to the business by banks, or corporate bonds, which are a special type of loan which can be traded between holders.
- Those that have lent the company money do not expect to be repaid in the short term, although do expect regular interest payments to be made, and of course for the amount loaned to be repaid as well in due course.
- We will explore sources of finance later in this book, just know for now that if it is due to be repaid in more than a years' time, it will appear here.

- A further example of a non-current liability that you may come across is pension liabilities. Pension accounting is very complicated, with calculations prepared by external advisors (actuaries) based on assumptions.

8   Current Liabilities

- **Current liabilities** are also known as Short-Term Liabilities, and these are amounts loaned to the company and which must be repaid in less than one year. As with current assets, there are a few common categories.
- **Payables** (also known as Creditors) is the opposite to the receivables we saw under assets. This is where a supplier has provided you with something, but you have not yet paid them. Usually this is by agreement (again 30 days delay is typical) but you may not be happy with the items delivered and have therefore held back payment. In general, it is better to hold onto cash longer, however this is increasingly seen as poor practice (especially when done by a large company to a smaller one) so care should be taken if deliberately not paying suppliers to the agreed terms. Payments due to tax authorities for payroll and social security taxes would also be shown here.
- **Accruals** and **Provisions** are another category of current liability. These arise where the company knows something is going to be due but has not yet had the invoice.
  - Accruals are usually more specific as they relate to a clear and expected invoice.
  - Provisions are more subtle, as they are made in anticipation of a cost arising, but the company may not be sure exactly when, or how much the cost might be.
  - This is clearly an area requiring careful judgement and should receive a high degree of focus from the finance team when it is being reported.
- The final category is **Bank Loans and Overdrafts**. This is where a bank has loaned the company some money, but it is repayable within 12 months (or even on demand). Accounting standards do not permit you to offset assets and liabilities, so it is not uncommon for a company to show both cash at bank and an overdraft, where they have multiple accounts.

9   Leasing

- It is, I think, appropriate to take a brief look at accounting for **leases**.
- Leasing is a very common form of finance for a company, enabling it to acquire and use an asset without paying for it up front or taking out a bank loan (see also Chapter 10). Leased assets are always tangible fixed assets.
- Historically there have been two types of leases:
  - Operating leases. These are for assets that are typically low value, are very common and frequently replaced. Good examples are photocopiers or computers.
  - Finance leases. These are for assets that usually have a higher value, might be more specialist and might be replaced less frequently. Almost any asset can be leased, but offices, vehicles factory equipment are all commonly leased.
- Until now there were complex rules for establishing which type of lease was in place, and once that was determined it would be accounted for differently depending upon whether it was an operating or a finance lease.
- However, that has recently changed, and a new standard (IRFS 16) was introduced in 2019. This requires all leases to be treated the same, and its relevance here is that leases affect both assets and liabilities.
- It can get complicated, so the key thing to know is that with a leased asset you will:
  - Recognise the initial value of the asset within the tangible fixed assets section. You will depreciate it over the estimated life of the asset (which is likely to be the same as the lease length, and certainly no longer)
  - Recognise a liability in both the current and non-current liabilities showing the lease payments that are due within 12 months (current) and beyond 12 months (non-current).
  - As the lease is paid, the liability will reduce, and the payments recorded in the Income Statement (split between operating expense and interest expense).

- This new standard has had a significant impact on the way results are reported by some companies, particularly those in industries with a high level of leased assets (such as retail and airlines) but almost all companies will be affected in some way.
- There are some exceptions for leased assets that are a very small value.
- Your finance team should be well versed in this and can explain how it is being managed in your company.

10   Equity

- The final Balance Sheet category is **Equity** (also known as Capital and Reserves). These are the amounts that have either been put into the business by the owners, or to which the owners are entitled to draw from the business.
- The owners of the business are known as **Shareholders** and each holds one or more shares in the company. In small businesses the shareholders and the people running the business day to day might be the same. In larger businesses (including those listed on the stock exchange) most of the shareholders are separate from the management activities.
- Companies will usually have Ordinary Shares, and these are shares initially issued when the company was set up. The shares have nominal value (the value written on the share certificate) and this is usually quite a small value (for example £1). The total number of shares issued and paid for multiplied by the nominal value is known as **Share Capital** and is shown first under Equity.
- Ordinary Shares are those that are most commonly traded on the stock exchange. However, the share price and the nominal value of a share should not be confused. The published share price is determined by the market and how many people want to buy or sell shares. As such it can go up or down, sometimes very quickly. The nominal value is fixed at the point of issue, and essentially never changes.
- Ordinary shareholders have certain rights to make decisions on how the company is run. These rights are set out in the Articles of Association (basically the rules of the company) and by Company Law. They exercise these rights by voting at meetings (the Annual General Meeting which must be held each year, or at an Extraordinary General Meeting).

- Ordinary shareholders may receive **dividends**, which is a form of interest paid by the company to those that have invested in it. Companies are not obliged to pay dividends although most do. It is an opportunity to return some of the profits made by the company to investors and is usually seen as a positive thing by shareholders.

- Sometimes companies issue Ordinary Shares at a value above the nominal value. In this case the excess over the nominal is known as Share Premium and this is usually shown next.

- Some companies also issue Preference Shares. These are similar to Ordinary Shares, except that they usually guarantee a dividend payment and usually have limited (or no) rights to vote at shareholder meetings.

- The final major category of reserves is known as Retained Reserves. Retained reserves are an accumulation of all the profits since the company was formed, less any dividends that have been distributed to shareholders over that same time. These are the residual profits that are available for distribution to the owners.

- Dividends are paid from the Retained Reserves and can only be paid if the company has made enough profit to pay a dividend. Dividends cannot be paid in anticipation of profits being made, and indeed it is illegal to pay or propose dividends that are higher than the retained reserves.

YOUR NOTES FROM CHAPTER 3

Chapter 4

Top 10 Tips for the Cash Flow Statement

In this chapter:

- What is a Cash Flow Statement?
- The layout of the Cash Flow Statement
- Key headings and what they contain
- How a Cash Flow Statement is prepared

The final primary statement in the accounts is called the Cash Flow Statement. It sometimes gets overlooked but is a vital part of understanding a company and its performance.

1   Cash Flow Statement

- Cash is a vital ingredient in keeping a company alive. Companies make losses from time to time, but often survive. However, a company can never survive if it runs out of cash.
- Thinking back to our apple tree, the flow of water from the roots of the tree, though the trunk to tip of the branches is essential for keeping the tree alive. If the water stops flowing, then the tree will surely die.
- Cash is the same. If there is not a supply of cash to allow the business to be funded, then it will very quickly wither and die.
- We will look at sources of funding in Chapter 10, as there are various ways in which a company can maintain a supply of cash.
- The Cash Flow Statement highlights these sources and shows the cash position at the end of the year and how that has moved from the previous year.
- Cash is also a key line in the Balance Sheet, and the cash flow statement must agree to the cash position shown there. The cash flow statement is designed to focus in detail on one aspect of the Balance Sheet.
- It is also true that cash is (or should be) a matter of fact. Whilst the Income Statement and Balance Sheet may contain judgements about what items are recognised and at what value, cash is a simple record of what is in a company's bank accounts. There is no judgement.

2   **Profit Versus Cash**

- You may think that because you have made a profit, you automatically must have more cash. This is not so.
- You will recall that accounts are prepared on an accruals basis. This means transactions are recognised when they occur, which may be very different to when the cash moves.
- For example: if I sell goods today but give my customer 60 days credit, I will recognise the sale in my Income Statement today, but the cash won't arrive for a further 2 months
- Or maybe I have just arranged a 3-year extended warranty on one of my assets and have paid for it today. The cash out would be recorded today, but the cost of the warranty would be spread out over 3 years in the Income Statement.
- In both these examples I might show a profit, but I would be short of cash.

3   **Layout**

- As with the other two primary statements that we have looked at, there is a layout that must be followed:

Cash Flow Heading	Notes
Cash from operating activities	*This can be worked out in two ways, see sections 5, 6 and 7*
Cash from/used by investing activities	*See section 8*
Cash from/used by financing activities	*See section 9*
Net increase/decrease in cash	*Sub-total: cash from operations + investing + financing*
Cash, cash equivalents and overdrafts at the beginning of the year	*From the opening Balance Sheet*
Cash, cash equivalents and overdrafts at the end of the year	*MUST EQUAL the closing Balance Sheet*

- Cash and cash equivalents shown at the bottom of the cash flow must agree to the figures shown in the Balance Sheet.

- Cash is the amount held in physical cash (for example as petty cash) plus anything held in a current account at a bank.
- Cash equivalents include amounts held in bank accounts that are readily available to the company. This is typically assumed to be savings accounts that can be accessed in less than 90 days, and where the savings are held for operational purposes and not as investments.
- Overdrafts are short term loans to the company, from a bank, that are repayable in the short term (often if the bank demands the company to do so).
- In combination these items represent the cash available to fund company activities.

4   Why Does the Cash Flow Statement get Overlooked?

- I mentioned at the start of this chapter that the cash flow sometimes gets overlooked.
- In my opinion this is because companies themselves sometimes play down its significance when talking about financial performance within the business and preparing management accounts.
- Cash does get a mention, but with less prominence than other measures.
- There is often a focus on the Income Statement, and indeed all internal performance reporting is generally centred around the Income Statement. Some companies may share the Balance Sheet as well on a regular basis, but few, in my experience, produce monthly Cash Flow Statements.
- This is partly because the Cash Flow Statement can be complicated to produce, and so few do so any more often than they must.
- Cash is sometimes seen as the preserve of the finance or treasury function and therefore not seen as something that the rest of the business needs to be involved with.
- However, as we shall see when we look at working capital in Chapter 6, the whole business can have a significant impact on cash and cash management.
- Therefore, I think more people should try to understand the Cash Flow Statement and what it is saying about the business performance.

5   Cash from operating activities

- The first section of the Cash Flow Statement sets out cash from operating activities.
- This shows the performance of the company in its day to day activities and whether it is generating (or spending) cash.
- Day to day activities include:
    - Cash from customers for goods or services sold to them.
    - Cash payments made to suppliers.
    - Payments made to employees (such as salaries, wages and expenses).
    - Interest payments made.
    - Tax payments made (or received).
- The slight complication is that there are two layouts permitted by the accounting standards (IFRS7) depending upon how the operating cash flow has been worked out. These are set out below.
- Whichever method is used, the calculation must be disclosed in the accounts.
- The two methods are:
    - The indirect method
    - The direct method

6   The Indirect Method of Calculation

- In my experience, the most common way of calculating the operating cash flow is the indirect method.
- The indirect method uses figures from the Income Statement and the Balance Sheet to work out what the operating cash flow was for the year.

- The following is a guide to how this is worked out:

Cash Flow Statement Heading	Notes
Profit before taxation	From the Income Statement
Adjustments for:	These are all non-cash items included in the Income Statement under accruals accounting
Depreciation	Add back
Foreign exchange gains/losses	Deduct gains, add back losses
Investment income	Deduct
Interest expense	Add back
Sub-total	
Changes in working capital	Calculated from the Balance Sheet
Movement in inventories	Deduct an increase, add back a decrease
Movement in receivables	Deduct an increase, add back a decrease
Movement in payables	Deduct a decrease, add back an increase
Cash generated from operations	Sub-total
Interest paid	Deduct the actual interest received in the year (not the Income Statement accrued value)
Tax paid/received	The actual tax paid or received in the year (not the Income Statement accrued value)
Net cash from operating activities	Sub-total

7   The Direct Method of Calculation

- This method is as valid as the one above, but one I have seen used less often.

- The direct method takes data from the source transactions (through the bank statement or cash book) and assigns them to categories.
- The following is a guide to how this is worked out:

Cash Flow Statement Heading	Notes
Cash received form customers	Worked out from bank statements
Cash paid to suppliers	Worked out from bank statements
Cash paid to and on behalf of employees	Worked out from bank statements
Cash generated from operations	Sub-total
Interest paid	Deduct the actual interest received in the year (not the Income Statement accrued value)
Tax paid/received	The actual tax paid or received in the year (not the Income Statement accrued value)
Net cash from operating activities	Sub-total

- Either method should come up with the same outcome, and so it should not really matter which you choose to use.
- The remainder of the Cash Flow Statement is the same regardless of how the operating cash flow has been derived.

8   **Investing Activities**

- Having identified the operating Cash Flow Statement, the next section sets out the investing activities of the organisation.
- Investing activities are those things that a company does with the longer-term interests of the company in mind (as opposed to short-term operational activities).

- This section of the Cash Flow Statement will commonly include some or all the following:
    - Acquisition or disposal of another company
    - Purchase of property, plant and equipment
    - Proceeds from the sale of equipment
    - Interest received (from bank deposits)
    - Dividends received (from shares held in other companies)
- It is important for readers of the accounts to understand how the business is investing in its future, and this is one area where this is highlighted.

9   Financing Activities

- Financing activities are those things company does to generate funds or to pay profits to shareholders.
- This section of the Cash Flow Statement will commonly include some or all the following:
    - Proceeds from the issuing of share capital
    - Proceeds from long-term borrowing
    - Repayments of long-term borrowing
    - Dividends paid to shareholders
- We will discuss raising funds in more detail in Chapter 10, but just be aware for now that many of the sources we discuss then will be shown here.

10   Balance Sheet Reconciliation

- As with the Income Statement, the Cash Flow Statement is shown for a period of time (for example the 12-months ended on a certain date).
- An important feature of the Cash Flow Statement is that it takes the total of cash and cash equivalents from a previous point in time and then shows the movement to get to the current position.
- Therefore, the last section of the Cash Flow Statement shows the cash balance at the start (usually the previous year-end) and then adds the movement in cash shown in the Cash Flow Statement to finish with the closing cash position, as per the Balance Sheet.
- This is neat and elegant, and a balancing Cash Flow Statement makes an accountant very happy indeed!

YOUR NOTES FROM CHAPTER 4

Chapter 5

Top 10 Tips for Understanding the Different Types of Accounts

In this chapter:

- The similarities and differences between financial accounts, management accounts and tax accounts
- The purpose of each
- The key questions that you should ask your finance team

In this chapter we are going to look at the different types of accounts, their features and what they are used for.

1   Types of Accounts

- We have talked about the primary financial statements (Income Statement, Balance Sheet and Cash Flow Statement) and these are used by all businesses to monitor and report their financial performance.
- However, there are three (and sometimes more) different types of accounts that are commonly used.
- These are management accounts, statutory accounts and tax accounts.
- Each of the types of accounts serve a slightly different purpose, although the fundamentals of the accounts are the same.

2   Different Types of Accounts and Their Purpose

	Financial Accounting	Management Accounting	Tax Accounting
Output	Annual report and accounts (Statutory Accounts)	Management accounts Internal reports	Tax return
Used by	External stakeholders	Internal stakeholders	Tax authorities
Published	Widely (eg Companies House, own website)	Internally Some external parties (such as banks or auditors)	No
Rules	Accounting standards Law / Other regulations Generally Accepted Accounting Principles	Set by the company, although usually will be prepared consistently with Financial Accounting	Accounting standards Law / Other regulations / GAAP Tax rules
Frequency	Annual 6 months for listed companies in the UK Legal deadlines for compliance	Monthly Deadline set by the company	Annual Legal deadlines for compliance
Comparisons	Prior year	Prior year Budget Forecast	None
Content	Income Statement/ Balance Sheet Cashflow (for large companies) Notes / Directors Report	Up to each company, but often: Income Statement / Balance Sheet Performance measures / Commentary	Tax return (Income Statement + Balance Sheet + Specific Information)
Audited	External audit	Internal audit (if applicable)	Partially – rely on audit of financial accounts Powers to investigate

| 3 | **Financial Accounting** |

- Financial accounting is the process of preparing financial information that will become widely available to stakeholders and the general public.
- The ultimate output is the annual report and accounts which are required to be produced by law or by other regulations.
- In the UK all companies must publish a report of business performance and the financial accounts annually, and all companies listed on the London Stock Exchange must produce accounts every 6 months.
- The annual report and accounts can be more than a hundred pages for the largest companies. Large companies must include [8]:
    - Highlights of the period being covered.
    - Strategic report.
    - Report on sustainability, ethics, values, and/or corporate and social responsibility.
    - Board of directors and secretary.
    - Corporate governance report.
    - Independent auditors' report (see Chapter 11).
    - Financial statements (accounts) for the year.
    - Shareholder information.
    - Financial calendar.
    - Company information.
    - Registrar and corporate advisors.
    - Glossary and reference to online information.
- The content for each area is strictly governed.
- We have discussed the primary financial statements, and these must be prepared for larger companies. In addition, there are other requirements, and together with the primary financial statements, these are sometimes known as the **statutory accounts**
    - Statements on comprehensive income and on changes in equity
    - Notes to the financial statements:
        - The notes to the financial statements provide more detail on the major items of the primary financial statements.
        - The notes will be cross-referenced from the relevant line of the primary statement.

- ▪ Not every line in a financial statement needs a note, but many of them will do.
- ▪ One of the first notes will be a statement of accounting policies, which summarises the main areas of judgements being made in the accounts, and how the company has approached these.
  - o A summary of the financial results for the previous 5 years.
- Guidance on the preparation of the strategic and corporate governance reports could be included in a separate book, (although we cover some aspects of governance in Chapter 11) but in outline they must include:
  - o An analysis of the company's performance.
  - o A description of the company's purpose, strategy and business model.
  - o A description of the principal risks and uncertainties facing the company.
  - o Information on gender diversity.
  - o Any other information that the Directors' considered to be useful to the reader of the report and accounts.
  - o A viability statement on the prospects for the business in the future, taking into consideration plans, risks and mitigations that can be made.
  - o Directors' remuneration.
- For smaller companies, or those that are not listed, the requirements are much less. Small companies need produce only abbreviated accounts. Companies that are not listed but are still large must produce more detailed accounts, but not the full set of requirements set out above. Many do choose to act as if they are listed and produce most of the same information. For example, John Lewis Partnership produce an annual report and accounts that would be almost identical if they were a listed company.
- For statutory accounts, the results for the current period are compared with those for the equivalent prior period. Budgets and forecasts are not usually published externally, and so these comparisons would not be available outside the company.

- The annual report and accounts must be published widely and in the UK this includes the Companies House website, which is the UK Government agency for companies. It is possible to look up the accounts for any company on their website, as well as information on directors, registered offices and so on. Most companies publish their accounts on their own website and distribute them to shareholders automatically.
- The annual report and accounts must be subject to an external audit as well, in the case of larger companies. We cover this in more detail in Chapter 11.
- The detail and complexity of the requirements means that the annual report and accounts can take several months to produce. They must be done within 6 months of the period end, and many companies will aim to have them completed in around 2 – 3 months.
- The interim accounts prepared by listed companies every 6 months are generally shorter than the annual accounts and will mainly be the primary financial statements plus some commentary.

4   Management Accounts

- Management accounts are used to manage the business day to day and month to month.
- They are usually produced monthly, and often compare the latest results to those of the same month the prior year and to budget or forecast (see Chapter 7).
- Commonly the information provided will have the performance for the latest month and the cumulative performance for the financial year to date.
- Most companies will produce a monthly Income Statement. Some, but not all, will produce a monthly Balance Sheet. In my experience, few produce a monthly Cash Flow Statement (although it is good practice to do so).
- Whilst the fundamentals of the accounts should be the same as the statutory accounts it is common for certain complex judgements to be ignored or simplified for the purposes of management accounts. For example, pension accounting is a notoriously difficult and volatile aspect, and most companies will ignore this in their management accounts.
- Variances to the prior year and to budget or forecast are often highlighted.

- Frequently a commentary is prepared to aid understanding of the results and to explain any variances.
- Typically, it can take between 5 and 15 working days to produce monthly management accounts. This depends on the size and complexity of the business, how many finance people are employed and the effectiveness of the processes around monthly reporting.
- Management accounts are primarily used inside the business, although it is common for certain external parties to ask to see them. Banks often ask for management accounts to be provided to them to aid their assessment of any loans or overdrafts that are being made. If a company is being considered for a take-over, then management accounts will usually be provided as part of the acquisition process.

5   Tax Accounts

- Most companies will have a separate set of accounts for the tax authorities. In the UK this is Her Majesty's Revenue and Customs (HMRC).
- HMRC is interested in the accounts, because they are seeking to levy a tax on the profits of the company (assuming there are profits). This known as **corporation tax**.
- Maintaining a different set of accounts is not because of any dubious or underhand activity by companies to hide profits from HMRC.
- There are legitimate reasons why the tax accounts might be different to the other accounts we have discussed. Most of the content will be the same, and indeed HMRC have taken steps over the years to ensure that should be the case. However, there are a few exceptions.
- The biggest exception, affecting almost every company, will be the treatment of depreciation (which we discussed as part of the Balance Sheet above).
  - o   HMRC have long felt that this is a highly subjective area for every company, and that there are incentives for companies to have a high depreciation charge to reduce their profits and therefore their tax bill.

- o To prevent this happening HMRC do not allow depreciation to be included in the accounts for the calculation of taxable profits.
- o Instead they allow what they call **capital allowances.**
- o Capital Allowances are very similar to depreciation in that they allow the company to recognise that assets are used in the business and that has a cost.
- o However, HMRC rules are much stricter and effectively force every company to use the same depreciation rates (Capital Allowances).
- o Hence there is a difference between the tax accounts and the other accounts.
- There are other differences as well, but a detailed analysis of these is outside the scope of this book. It is enough to say there are some valid reasons for have differences between the tax accounts and the others, but these differences should always be understood and explained by reference to HMRC rules rather than fraudulently failing to disclose profits.

6   Why are my Finance Colleagues Always Busy?

- Looking at the sets of accounts we have discussed, you start to get a sense of why finance teams often seem to be busy.
- There are likely to be twelve month end processes to prepare the management accounts, each of which might take 2 weeks or more.
- There will then be annual reporting requirements and for listed companies 6 monthly reporting requirements as well. Both are in more depth and take longer to produce.
- So, you can see that for most finance teams more than half their year is taken with reporting requirements. Add in support for Budgeting and Forecasting (see Chapter 7) and it is easy to see why finance teams are often working to a deadline.

7   What Information Should I Get?

- To an extent, how information is shared in your business is unique to you. Different companies take different approaches to this, and it might also depend upon your role and responsibilities in the organisation.
- However, it should always be possible to see the statutory accounts for your company, even if you must look them up for yourself on the Companies House website.
- If you have responsibility for an area, department or business unit then you should be able to see the Management Accounts for your part of the business.
- Companies will often share the financial performance of the business monthly or quarterly with all their employees, although sometimes this will be done in broad terms to avoid revealing confidential or share price sensitive information.

8   What is in it for Me?

- I think that understanding the financial performance of the company is an essential part being an effective employee. By understanding the financial aspect of the business and how they inform and reflect decision making everyone becomes more efficient and is better able to contribute.
- One case study for this has been set out by Jack Stack and Bo Burlingham [9].
- They tell the story of a factory which was in significant financial difficulty, but by ensuring everyone had a good grasp of the finances and the impact they could have on the business by understanding these, they were able to turn the factory into a success even in difficult economic times.
- Part of their success was educating the whole workforce about the finances of the factory and ensuring they all understood the impact they could have on the results.
- The management team also ensured that the finances were a core part of all their discussions, including weekly updates on performance and forecasts.

9   Questions to Ask my Finance Colleagues

- I think three key questions that you should ask to improve your understanding of the financial performance of your area or business, and its impact.
- They are questions that can be used in lots of situations to unlock constructive dialogue and understanding, but here we focus on the finance aspects.
- The three key questions are:
  - What has happened?
  - What assumptions have been made?
  - What does this mean for the business going forwards?
- You will note each of the questions is an open question, which will likely bring out a broader range of analysis than closed questions.

I.   What has happened?
  - The purpose of this question is to get a common understanding of the current situation.
  - You might be given an answer that compares an actual outcome to a budget or forecast, to a prior period or to some other expectation.
  - It may just be a statement of fact as to what the situation is and its impact on the Income Statement, Balance Sheet or Cash Flow Statement.

II.   What assumptions have been made?
  - The purpose of this question is to get greater depth or understanding about the situation.
  - Almost all accounting involves some assumptions, be it around timing, value involved, likely outcome and so on.
  - Therefore, understanding the assumptions that are being made is vital to understanding the situation.
  - It may not be the finance tram making these assumptions. They may have been provided with information form others in the business and will have taken that into consideration. Therefore, this question is as much about checking alignment of understanding. Bear in mind, it might have been you that provided the information, so it is worth checking it has been interpreted correctly!

III. **What does this mean for the business going forwards?**

- o This question will then help to understand the impact of the situation and assumptions on the business going forwards.
- o This may be just in the form of understanding how the financial results will be reported in the future.
- o However, it may also involve decisions that need to be made to allow the business to capitalise on an opportunity or to mitigate a risk.

10   What Actions Can I Take?

- My recommendations for what you can do to take positive steps to engage with your finance colleagues are as follows.
- Reflect on what you have learned from this book (and I realise we are only halfway through!).
- Have active discussions with your finance colleagues:
  - o Get to understand what they are working on.
  - o Explain what you do, and how you can work together.
  - o Ask the key questions.
- Don't shy away from getting involved in the finances of your business – it is important for everyone to understand how it all works and how they can contribute to the financial success of the company.

YOUR NOTES FROM CHAPTER 5

Chapter 6

Top 10 Tips for Monitoring Money In and Money Out

In this chapter:

- How expenditure can be controlled
- The working capital cycle
- Management of cash

We have looked at the Cash Flow Statement as primary financial statement (see Chapter 4). In this section we look at the practical aspects of managing cash in a business in the short and medium term.

1   Authority to Spend

- When an employee of a company makes a promise to buy some goods or services from someone else, and if someone else reasonably believes that employee has authority, then that promise is binding on the company. Therefore, care must be taken when making commitments to buy things on behalf of your business.
- Unless you are in a very small business, it is likely that your company has a process that sets out what you can commit the company to spending money on, by type of expenditure and value limit.
- This is often called **delegation of authority matrix**.
- Most delegations of authority set out by category of spend what the authority limits are, usually by level of the organisation. For example:
  - A department manager has authority to spend £5,000 in any one transaction on day to day items.
  - A functional head has authority to spend £50,000 on day to day items.
  - Above £50,000 the CEO or CFO must authorise the expenditure.
  - All capital expenditure must be authorised by the CFO, regardless of value.
- These are just illustrations: companies are free to set their own limits that balance the need to control cash out with the need to efficiently process business transactions.
- It is important for you to find out what the delegation of authority matrix is for your company.

2   Purchase Order Process

- A lot of larger companies use a purchase order process in order to allow effective control of expenditure before it is committed, and efficient processing of payments once the goods or services have been delivered.
- A typical process is as follows [10]:

- The first stage is to identify what it is the business needs to purchase.
- Sometimes this will be formalised by the creation of a purchase requisition, that sets out the requirement and business justification.
- This would then be approved, commonly by referring to the delegation of authority matrix.
- Once approved, a supplier will be identified.
  - This might be a supplier already pre-selected to provide these types of good or services.
  - If a new item is being purchased a different supplier might be needed.

- A **purchase order** (also known as a PO) will then be created.
  - The PO sets out the specification of the items being requested from the supplier, the quantity and price, the delivery address and payment terms. It will also have a unique identification number, which the supplier should then quote when they invoice for the goods or services.
  - In certain circumstances supplier contracts might be negotiated centrally and a blanket PO created. This might cover a range of commonly purchased items up to an annual value. Stationary is a common example. This avoids repeatedly generating POs for frequently used things.
- The PO will then be authorised, again in line with the delegation of authority matrix, and sent to the supplier as evidence of what has been requested.
- When the goods and services have been delivered, someone in the company with knowledge of what has been provided should raise a **goods receipt note** (also known as GRN).
  - The purpose of the GRN is to acknowledge that the goods or services have been received, and that they have been delivered in the quantity and quality specified in the order. It is accepting that the supplier can now raise an invoice.
  - The raising of a GRN will usually initiate the accruals accounting of the cost, as it is a trigger to say the company has a committed liability.
  - It might be that the goods or services have only partially been delivered. This is fine, provided you only raise a GRN for what has been delivered. The remainder of the PO will be held open until the entire order is completed.
- Sometimes there is a difference between the order and the delivery. How this gets handled will depend upon the situation, but any increase in price or quantity over the original order will probably require the whole order to be authorised again. This will cause delays in processing the invoice.
- After delivery of the goods or services, the supplier will send in an invoice. Many companies insist that suppliers quote their purchase order number on the invoice, and without this the invoice will not be paid. If this is your company, then you need to make that clear to the supplier.

- If the invoice matches the GRN, which in turn matched the PO, then the invoice can be swiftly processed, and the supplier paid on schedule. This is called a three-way match (invoice = GRN = PO).
- If the invoice does not match the GRN then delays can occur. If the invoice is less than the GRN by quantity or value, then many companies will just pay on the assumption the supplier has raised a partial invoice. Any subsequent invoice will be checked to make sure the GRN value is not exceeded.
- If the invoice is higher than the GRN then invoice will be delayed. The invoice is higher than the approved amount, and therefore a new invoice will need to be raised for a lower amount or a new authorisation sought for a higher amount.

3 Opex

- We have previously discussed opex as part of the Income Statement in Chapter 2.
- Opex is an abbreviation of operating expenses, and these are the day to day costs of running a business.
- As such they can be many and varied, from routine costs such as electricity or stationery through to significant expenditure on machinery repairs or marketing campaigns.
- The approval to spend opex is usually subject to a relatively straightforward process, such as the purchase order process set out above.
- Delegation to spend is permitted by value and usually restricted to the immediate business area that you are working in. This is commonly known as a **cost centre** (which we also looked at in Chapter 1).
- Some companies also include the budget as part of the approval process. We talk about budgeting in Chapter 7, but sometimes the inclusion of a cost item in a budget makes the approval of spending that money more straightforward. Conversely, approval to spend money not anticipated in the budget might involve additional steps of justification and authorisation.

4   Capex

- Capex is an abbreviation of capital expenditure, and we looked this earlier as part of the Balance Sheet. Capex is purchase of assets that will be used in the business for more than a year. You will recall that the cash impact of capex is felt in the near term, but the Income Statement impact is spread over several years as the depreciation is recorded.

- Companies frequently have separate, and more complex authorisation processes for capex. This is because the sums of money involved are frequently larger than for opex, and the impact on the business will be seen for a much longer period.

- It is often the case that there are multiple capex projects that a company is considering, but that it cannot afford to do all of them. Therefore, there needs to be a method of establishing which project is better than another. This is called investment appraisal.

- There are three common **investment appraisal** techniques. Your company may use all of them, a subset or indeed none of them.

- We will discuss them briefly here, but my usual advice to anyone approaching this area is to work closely with your finance team as you are developing a capex proposal. The concepts here can be complex, and unless you are in a company that does a lot of capex, may not be something you use frequently.

- The first method is **payback period**.
  - This is the simplest tool. It simply measures how long it takes to recover the value of the initial investment from increased profits and cash generated.
  - The shorter the period to recover the initial investment the better the project.
  - However, this can penalise projects that have a better overall opportunity to generate cash in the long term, and therefore in my experience is rarely the only tool used.

- The second method is **net present value** (also known as **NPV**).
  - This compares the initial investment with the cash expected to be generated over the whole life of equipment acquired.

- A critical difference between this and the payback period is that the calculation considers the time value of money, by working out a **discounted cash flow**.
- The time value of money is a recognition that £1 today is worth less in the future. A major factor is inflation (think about what £1 buys you today compared with 10 years ago) but for a business there is also the fact that there will be some financing cost of raising cash for the investment and a risk that it might not work out as planned.
- All these factors are wrapped up in what is called the **cost of capital** for the business.
- Each company will have its own cost of capital based on a variety of factors, but something around 10% is common. This is known as the discount rate.
- The future cash flows are then reduced by the discount rate.
- Once this has been done, all the future cash flows are added together, and the initial investment deducted. This gives the NPV.
- If the NPV is negative, then the cash flows will not cover the investment and the project should not proceed.
- If the NPV is positive, then the project is expected to generate more cash than the investment.
- The greater the NPV the better the project.

- The final method is called the **internal rate of return** (also known as **IRR**).
  - This is in effect a variation of the NPV but expresses the return from a project as a percentage.
  - The assumptions around cash flows and discount rate are similar.
  - The IRR percentage is compared with the cost of capital.
  - If the IRR is greater than the cost of capital, then the project is a good one and is expected to generate wealth for the company.

- A really important point in all three methods is the importance surrounding the assumptions being made, especially around future cash flows. The initial investment should be reasonably well known, but the future is less certain. The additional cash flow will be derived from:
    - Additional sales revenue, leading to additional profits
    - Reduced costs through efficiency of operations
- It is important to make the assumptions realistic, and frequently different scenarios will be explored as part of the appraisal process. Getting the assumptions wrong might mean making the wrong investment which could have an adverse impact on the company.
- Furthermore, companies will often set targets for payback period, NPV and IRR. If a project does not meet the required target, then it will not be considered for approval.
- Whilst we are not going to go into a great deal of detail, a simple example illustrates how this may be applied in practice:
    - Two proposals have been put forwards, each of which cost £1,000 to invest in and will provide income for five years
    - You are told the cost of capital for the company is 10%
    - Project A is assumed to generate £1,400 as follows:

2020	2021	2022	2023	2024	Total
500	400	200	200	100	**1,400**

- Project B is assumed to generate £1,600 as follows:

2020	2021	2022	2023	2024	Total
100	200	200	400	700	**1,600**

- Which would you invest in?

- The investment appraisal tools suggest the following:

	Project A		Project B	
	Cash flow	**Discounted**	**Cash flow**	**Discounted**
	(1,000)	(1,000)	(1,000)	(1,000)
2020	500	455	100	91
2021	400	331	200	165
2022	200	150	200	150
2023	200	137	400	273
2024	100	62	700	435
TOTAL	**1,400**	**1,134**	**1,600**	**1,114**
Payback	2.50		4.14	
NPV		134.1		114.3
IRR		16.8%		13.3%

- In this example, both projects would be beneficial to the company as they pay back in the near term and have positive NPVs and IRRs greater than the 10% cost of capital.
- However, if forced to choose between the two, Project A is better as it pays back sooner and has a higher NPV and IRR.

5 The Working Capital Cycle

- The **working capital** cycle describes how money moves through the business in the normal course of its day to day operations.
- Money is generated from sales but can get stuck if the business is not paid quickly enough. In the meantime, the business will be making payments to suppliers, employees and so on, and will also be holding stocks of goods ready for sale. These elements make up the working capital cycle.

- This can be illustrated as follows:

Inventories: stocks of raw materials and finished goods that have not yet been sold

Accounts receivable: sales made to customers, where the cash has not yet been received

Accounts payable: goods and services received from suppliers, but which we have not yet paid

- Working capital management involves getting cash in from customers more quickly, holding the lowest amount of inventory possible and delaying payments to suppliers for as long as possible.
- If insufficient cash is generated form sales to cover the costs of running the business and the inventories being held, then alternative funding will be required (see Chapter 10).

6   Getting Cash in From Customers

- It is vital that companies have effective processes to collect cash from customers as soon as possible. This is the most effective way for a company to generate cash.
- Often companies will offer customers credit terms, of, for example, 30 days. This means that there will be a delay of 30 days before you receive any money, despite having provided the services.
- The shorter the credit terms the better it is for you, the company making the sale.

- Even if you have agreed terms, it is sadly a common occurrence that your customers won't pay until after the agreed time. Therefore, you should take steps to actively control your customer receipts:
  - Agree the shortest possible payment terms with customers.
  - Make sure you deliver goods and services as specified and to the required quality.
  - Make sure you comply with any administrative requirements of the customer. This may be the way the invoice is submitted, the need to quote a purchase order number and so on.
  - Be prepared to contact the customer *before* the invoice is due, to make sure it has gone through all the necessary processes and is ready to be paid.
  - As soon as an invoice is late, contact the customer and chase for payment, and don't give up until the invoice is settled. This may involve withholding future sales until the invoice is paid. This is a difficult decision, as it may jeopardise future revenue, but there is no such thing as a good customer that does not pay their bills!
- Where this a significant risk for a company, there will usually be a formal credit control department within the finance function, tasked with following these steps.
- The metric commonly used to monitor performance in this area is called Days Sales Outstanding (DSO). This is a calculation of the average amount of time it takes to convert an invoice to a cash payment, expressed in the number of days.

$$\text{Days Sales Outstanding (DSO)} = \frac{\text{Debtors}}{\text{12 months' Sales}} \times 365$$

- If your payment terms are 30 days and your DSO is also 30 days, then you are collecting to time.
- If your DSO is, for example, 55 days then you are being too slow to collect payments, and this could cause issues of funding.

7   Managing Inventories

- Inventories are stocks of materials that you are holding ready for sale.
- There are 3 main types of inventory:
  - Raw materials: these are components that you have acquired in anticipation of turning them into products in the future.
  - Work in progress: this is where some activities have been carried out and the products are partially finished, but not yet ready to be sold to customers. It includes raw materials form above but also the time and expenses of assembling the products to this stage. Service companies can also have work in progress, where they have delivered some of the service but not yet invoiced for it.
  - Finished goods: this is the completed product, ready to be shipped out to customers. It includes all raw materials and assembly costs.
- The value of inventory is greater at the finished goods stage than at the raw material stage. However, finished goods are nearer to being ready for sale and therefore realising cash than raw materials.
- The shorter the time it takes from acquiring and assembling raw materials to selling them to customers the better. Cash is tied up while goods are held in inventory and cannot be used to pay suppliers or invest in the business.
- As with receivables, there are steps to be taken to manage inventory:
  - Properly assess what you need and only buy in raw materials as you need them. The ultimate expression of this is 'just in time' manufacturing, which is prevalent in many industries now. Raw materials are delivered to the final assembly factory just as they are required, almost eliminating inventory.
  - Matching sales and production helps minimise finished goods inventory. This can be a difficult thing to achieve, but if there are accurate sales forecast then the factory can produce only what is required, when it is required. Even better if items are produced only to order, and the customer is invoiced as soon as the item is completed.

- o Prompt invoicing of customers when goods are delivered is important. It also helps to take a deposit from the customer before any work is started and this will help generate cash. Whether this can be done in your industry is a matter of custom and practice as much as anything else.
- There is a measure of effectiveness known as Days Inventory Outstanding (DIO).

$$\text{Days Inventory Outstanding (DIO)} = \frac{\text{Inventory}}{\text{12 months' Cost of Sales}} \times 365$$

- This expresses the value of the inventory being held in terms of the number of days' worth of production. In general, the lower the DIO the better for working capital.

8   Payments to Suppliers

- The final part of the working capital cycle are payments being made to suppliers.
- Certain suppliers require frequent payments, without fail. Employees will not stick around long if you do not pay them weekly or monthly as per their contracts. Similarly, energy and communications companies and the tax authorities take a dim view of not being paid promptly and they have sufficient leverage to make life very difficult if not paid.
- However, other suppliers will often offer payment terms that allow you to delay paying them. For example, they might offer you 30 days terms (like the credit you might offer to customers as we saw earlier).
- The longer the terms the better for you, and the worse for the supplier who also needs to consider their working capital. Money owed by you to a supplier is an interest-free loan.

- Such payment terms are negotiable between the parties, and longer terms may be agreed to secure business from you. However, you should be aware that these negotiations are not always between equals. Where a large company is buying from a smaller one, the smaller one might feel pressured to accept longer terms.

- I am also aware that sometimes larger companies unilaterally change their payment terms to the detriment of the supplier, on the assumption that the supplier will just accept it. I once received such a letter and we quickly decided not to deal with that company going forwards, unless the previous terms were reinstated.

- I am always an advocate of paying suppliers to the terms that have been agreed. It is morally questionable to delay payments, unless there is genuine dispute between the parties as to what is due.

- Since 2018, large companies in the UK have been required to publish their payment practices on a government website. This is to highlight how the company treats its suppliers and to allow them to decide on whether to supply the company or not. It is a self-reporting tool, and so needs some caution but at least it is better than nothing.

- As with the other working capital items, there is a measure to track payables. It is called Days Payable Outstanding (DPO) and expresses the value of amounts owed in terms of days of purchases.

$$\text{Days Payable Outstanding (DPO)} = \frac{\text{Creditors}}{\text{12 months' Cost of Sales}} \times 365$$

- In general, the higher the DPO the better it is for working capital.

9   **Cash Conversion Cycle**

- Together the three elements of the working capital cycle can be combined to show the cash conversion cycle (CCC) as follows:

Cash conversion cycle (in days) = DSO + DIO – DPO

- If a business is performing well and is efficiently serving the needs of the market and its customers, it will have a lower CCC value.
- Usually the CCC is tracked over multiple periods of time to understand if working capital needs are improving or deteriorating.
- In isolation the working capital requirements can vary between industries quite significantly depending upon the nature of the business activity. Where an industry has higher working capital requirements, then you would reasonably expect the profits to be higher to compensate for the greater risk of cash being tied up in operations.

10   **Supporting Cash Management in my Company**

- There are several things you may be able to do to ensure that money and money out is managed effectively.
- Check what processes are in place in your company to manage purchases and payments, and make sure you adhere to them.
- Work closely with your finance team on all aspects of opex, capex and working capital.
- Where you are directly involved in supplying goods and services to customers, make sure that you do so efficiently and line with customer expectations.
- Look at ways to make more effective use of cash in your business area.

YOUR NOTES FROM CHAPTER 6

Chapter 7

Top 10 Tips for Business Planning, Budgeting and Forecasting

In this chapter:

- Why do businesses create business plans?
- What is the difference between a business plan, a budget and a forecast?
- How do the processes work?

So far, our focus has mainly been on reporting historical performance: a backwards look at what has happened for the business in the past. In this chapter we examine the way businesses look to the future, through business planning, setting budgets and making revised forecasts.

1   Budgets and Business Plans

- Small businesses often survive without any detailed plans. The owner or main shareholder knows the business well enough, and can direct any employees that they may have to meet the objectives of the business
- However, as businesses grow there is an inevitable increase in complexity, and it is common for governance structures to be set up to support the delivery of business objectives.
- Setting a budget is a very common part of the governance of most businesses. It allows resources to be allocated, plans to be communicated, targets to be set and performance to be assessed.
- Budgets are usually set for 12 months ahead, aligned to financial year of the business.
- It is common for budgets to be worked up over several months, for approval by the main Board 4 to 8 weeks before the start of that financial year.
- Larger businesses will set the budget in the context of a longer-term business plan. Business plans are typically set for 3 to 5 years ahead and will explore the options available to the company to deliver its objectives in the medium term.
- Year 1 of the business plan becomes the budget for that first year.
- Forecasts are carried out during the financial year.
- Forecasts provide an update on the performance of the business (usually against budget) for the current year, and sometimes are used to provide some guidance on subsequent years.

- Forecasts are often carried out quarterly, but in some cases might be required every month of the year.

2   Stakeholders for Budgets

- Business plans, budgets and forecasts are very much internal documents, primarily aimed at being used within the company that prepares them.
- Frequently senior managers in the business use these as tools to understand performance, but also to set targets including those that might lead to bonuses for employees.
- The budget is a common comparator for the management accounts (see Chapter 5) so that the month and year to date performance are compared to the budget. Often the forecast is used in the same way, as well as or instead of the budget.
- It is also common for certain external stakeholders to see these, on the understanding that they are confidential as they often include plans that the company would not want competitors to see.
  - These external stakeholders include banks, financial advisors and external auditors.
- Since they are often used as a tool for communication, performance management and bonus setting, then of course all employees should have a keen interest in the targets for their area and play a role in understanding and developing them where appropriate.

3   Budgeting

- As I mentioned, the **budget** is usually set for the next 12 months (the financial year).
- A budget should be set for all three primary financial statements: Income Statement, Balance Sheet and Cash Flow Statement.
- As it is a look to the future, there inevitably some estimates, judgements and indeed guesses being made about what might happen. A good budget process involves highlighting these for discussion at key points of the process.

- For the Income Statement, the key areas of focus are usually:
  - Sales volume.
  - Average sales price.
  - The mix of products being sold.
  - Production costs.
  - Sales and marketing expenditure.
  - Overhead expenditure.
  - Finance costs (for example loan interest).
- For the Balance Sheet, the focus is frequently on:
  - Capital expenditure plans.
  - Working capital assumptions.
- The Cash Flow Statement is usually derived from the information above and will be looked at to assess the funding requirements for the business, and what it can afford to invest in the future or pay out in dividends.
- Budgeting is usually done in detail, with projections made for each individual month. This is particularly useful to allow the business to reflect any seasonal fluctuations that may exist for sales or production.
- Individual departments often take responsibility for budgeting the items in their area (for example sales will lead the budgeting of sales volumes and selling prices).
- Budget holders are often called cost centre managers, particularly where the function is an overhead expense.
- However, it is essential in any budgeting process that departments work together and coordinate their budgets. For example, it is no good the sales department preparing a budget that has a higher level of production than can be manufactured by the production department. A common problem area in this regard is where production takes place in one country, but sales are in another, and coordination between the various parts of the business needs to be carefully managed.

- A typical budget process looks like this:

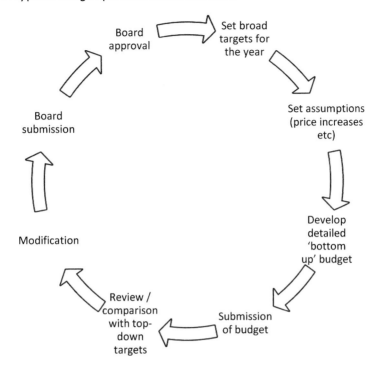

- Most budget processes start with the setting of broad targets for the year ahead. These may be based on the current year performance, expectations from shareholders or some other reference point. Good budget processes involve these being shared with those in the organisation that will be tasked with preparing the detail.
- These broad targets are often limited in detail and might be restricted to revenue and profit.
- Certain broad assumptions will then be set, to allow for some commonality amongst the budget-setters. Businesses will have different assumptions, but common ones are:
  - o Salary and wage increases.
  - o Inflation.
  - o Production capacity.
  - o Capital expenditure.
  - o Foreign exchange rates.

- The relevant budget holders or departments will then be tasked with preparing their detailed plans. This is commonly called the 'bottom up' part of the process, as it is prepared at the most detailed level for the organisation.
  - As we have already noted, this is where coordination between departments can be essential. I would also recommend that this is a stage at which you engage closely with your local finance team.
  - They can help you pull together the details that are required and should be able to provide you with support and advice as you work through the process.
- The bottom up budget is usually submitted to a central finance team, often in a standard format to allow all the detailed budgets to be quickly brought together.
- There would then normally be a review process. Often this is in the form a meeting with the head of the business unit, and for those companies with several layers of management, there may be multiple review meetings.
- These review meetings will often compare the budget to the top-down targets established at the beginning of the process.
- There should also be a focus on the judgements and estimates that have been made so that they are widely understood and agreed.
- This is the stage at which budgets often go through multiple iterations, as the review process challenges assumptions and changes are made to reflect this.
- Eventually, you will end up with an agreed budget covering the whole organisation, which is submitted to the main Board of the company (in the UK, this will include the Chair and non-executive directors). This should have been thoroughly examined and be representative of the views of everyone involved.
- The Board will tend to look at the budget at higher level and are unlikely to look at the detail (although they will expect the detailed work to have been done).
  - Instead, they will focus on key areas and certain performance indicators.
  - The Board should challenge the executive directors on the content of the budget and be satisfied that is a sensible projection of the business. They will ultimately approve the budget.

4   **Budgeting Approaches**

- I am frequently asked what the outcome of a good budget process should be. To my mind the following are an essential part of any budget process:
    - o   The final budget should have targets that are _stretching but achievable_. This means they should have some ambition in them, and therefore might show a performance level higher than is currently being achieved but should not be so difficult that the targets cannot be reached.
    - o   Everyone involved in the process should be properly engaged with the budget and should feel that the budget in their area is something that they recognise and 'own'.
    - o   The budget process should be transparent and open so that an honest assessment of the likely business performance can be established and tested.
- However, within these parameters there are two common approaches that I have come across to budgeting.
- The first, and most common in my experience, is to start with some known information, typically recent actual performance combined with a reasonable forecast for the rest of the current financial period.
    - o   This is then extrapolated to the budget year, adjusting for assumptions or known changes in the business.
    - o   There is frequently a challenge target added to the extrapolated figures before the budget is finalised and this is a common point of discussion between budget holders and management.
    - o   The advantage of this method is that it is relatively quick and easy to develop the budget.
- The second method is to use the zero-based budgeting method.
    - o   In this approach the budget is built up from scratch, ignoring previous assumptions, and therefore explores the targets and options afresh.
    - o   This can allow businesses to look at their operating activities in different ways, consider new practices and to an extent ignore embedded efficiencies and inefficiencies.
    - o   However, this approach can be significantly more time-consuming than the extrapolation method.

- In practice, many companies use a hybrid of both approaches, with much of the budget built up from historic activities, but some aspects (particularly new or changing activities) established from a zero base.

5 Business Planning

- Many businesses, particularly larger ones, have medium-term business plans that typically cover the next 3 to 5 years.
- The purpose of a business plan is to reflect and inform some of the strategic decisions that are facing the business.
- A good business plan will include consideration of all the primary financial statements, although typically in much less detail than the actual results (and budget).
- There should be a close link between the strategic plan (see below) and the business plan. In that sense the business plan as providing detail that reflects the strategic thinking of the business and its management.
- Good business plans will include much more than just financial metrics and will often cover a range of other operational metrics.
- The first year of the business plan is usually the budget.

6 Strategic Planning

- Whilst not purely a finance matter, there is and should be a close link between a business' strategic plan and business plan.
- We are not going to discuss strategy in detail in this book (there are a lot of strategy books available) but I think worth a brief overview so that you can see how strategy, business planning and budgeting fit together.
- A strategy is about:
  - A set of choices as to what *to do* or *not to do* to address:
    - Desired outcomes for the business.
    - Which markets to compete in.
    - Products or service being offered.
    - Customers being targeted.
    - Geography that is operated in.
    - The value proposition we are offering (why would someone buy from our company?).
  - Building *long-term* sustainable *competitive advantage*.
  - Doing better than the *industry average*.

- o *Balance* long-term view with short-term targets.
- o The creation of a *unique*/differentiated position.
- Typically, a strategy process follows a loop such as this:

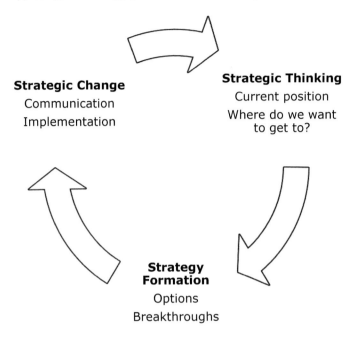

Strategic Change
Communication
Implementation

Strategic Thinking
Current position
Where do we want
to get to?

**Strategy
Formation**
Options
Breakthroughs

- Current position involves looking at what is going on inside and outside of the business and assessing the trends that might have an impact in the future.
- Companies will then look to evaluate the various options that might be available in the medium-term (which are usually much wider than those that can be considered in the near-term) and develop those plans into a strategy.
- This strategy then needs to be communicated across the business so that is can be implemented effectively and consistently. This is the stage that in my view is often the most difficult and most overlooked in many companies.

- The elements of a good strategic plan are as follows:
  - Having a documented plan that has evaluated the environment and has clearly articulated the choices made.
  - Clearly identifying the resources required to deliver the chosen plan.
  - The risks and opportunities associated with the plan are made clear.
    - Risks are those things that might happen to prevent the plan being achieved, and as well as being identified plans to mitigate them should be explored.
    - Similarly, there may be opportunities to outperform the plan, and these should be clear with an explanation as to how they might be delivered.
  - There should be clear performance measures to assess the success of the strategy.
    - Commonly these will be financial and will be reflected in the business plan.
    - However, there may also be non-financial measures.
  - The plan should be clear, concise and the communication of the plan to the wider organisation should be engaging.

7   Forecasting

- Forecasting is usually a term for a reassessment of the performance of the business during the year.
- Typically, a **forecast** involves taking the financial performance of the business in the financial year to date, and then projecting the outcome over the time remaining to the end of the year.
- Usually forecasts are prepared in a similar level of detail to the budget with a month by month projection of what might happen.
- In my experience forecasts are usually performed two or three times a year.
- The purpose is to provide information to the management as to how the business is tracking against expectations (usually those set in the budget) so that this can be communicated and if necessary new decisions made.

- Commonly, the projection aspect of the forecast is based on the budget, updated for new information. This cuts down some of the time required to develop a forecast.
- Care needs to be taken where the timing of activities has changed so that these are not missed or double counted when pulling together the forecast.

8   What Do I need to Do?

- I recommend the following approach to budgeting, particularly if you are new to the organisation or department or have never had budget responsibility before.
- Firstly, get to know who your finance contact is. Many companies assign responsibilities to the finance team to partner with certain individuals or departments. They are an invaluable resource to help you, so it is worth getting to know them.
- Understand what areas you are going to be expected to prepare a budget for. This could be a whole business unit or department or just one or two cost centres.
- Get to know what is included in those costs centres that you have responsibility for. What income or cost is usually included? Many companies assign costs for things like shared office space, IT equipment or phones; is that the case in your company?
- If it is new area for you, develop an understanding of what is driving the financial performance and what you can do to positively influence the outcomes.
- You should also understand how your area fits in with the overall objectives of the business.
- Finally, it can be helpful to look at what other companies are doing, whether they are in the same industry or not. It is often beneficial to benchmark your performance against those of others. Using some of the ratios set out in the next chapter might be helpful.

9   Common Pitfalls

- There are a few issues with budgeting and forecasting. These are common to many organisations and I have certainly seen them all to one degree or another.
- Budgeting and forecasting processes can be hugely time consuming. Whilst much of this burden often falls on the finance team, it can involve a lot of the business focused on the process of establishing and negotiating the budget outcome.
  - This may be seen as a distraction from the actual day to day activity of running the business, even though the budget is usually accepted as being an important process.
  - Companies often see the budget process as a discrete project, albeit one that occurs annually, and it can be all-consuming during key times of preparation and review.
- This time can be exacerbated where there has not been early alignment between the expectations of the most senior management, and those who are preparing the budget.
  - Sometimes the top-down view is one of higher performance (be that sales, profit, cash or whatever) than the bottom-up budget has set out.
  - This can cause a lot of discussion, and potentially many iterations of the budget, all of which takes time.
- There are occasions where a budget can date very quickly, due to internal or external events. I recall preparing a budget for a manufacturing business in late 2008, as the recession was taking hold in the UK. Sales fell so quickly that just a few weeks later we had to prepare a whole new budget, almost from scratch. Where a budget process takes a long time, this problem is likely to be worsened.
- Sometimes budgets are seen as a constraint rather than a target. Once the budget holder has met their budget for the year, they might sit back and wait for the next financial year to come around.
- Another pitfall is that budget processes can become a bit of a game. It can be seen as successful to have got away with setting a budget that is easier than it could have been. This can then lead to rewards for performance that is only adequate, or to a constraint being set lower than it might have been.

- This might manifest itself more subtly by creating some slack or padding in the budget. This involves including some cost that might not happen or excluding income that is almost certain. If this is not highlighted (or spotted) during the review and approval process, then budget is flawed.
- Finally, I have often come across confusion about which is benchmark against which performance should be measured.
  - At the start of the year, most people are clear that it should be against budget.
  - However, as forecasts are submitted there can be a tendency to want to use those instead, especially if performance is falling short budget.
  - Each organisation will handle this differently, but my view has always been that the budget is the primary reference point, and the forecast is merely providing guidance as to what the actual outcome is likely to be.

10   Alternative Approaches

- Some organisations have sought out ways to mitigate these pitfalls.
- One option is to have a rolling budget or forecast.
  - This involves updating the outlook, usually for the next 12 months, more frequently.
  - The latest information is incorporated as a matter of course.
  - Rolling budgets or forecasts can be prepared monthly or quarterly.
  - This takes the budget away from being an annual project and instead brings it into a more regular routine. It becomes a habit.
  - It is debateable, in my view, if this saves any time in practice.
- Another is to not do budgets at all.
  - There is a movement called Beyond Budgeting [11], which advocates that the pitfalls are too great to overcome, and that businesses can work more effectively without budgets

- o The focus is on using performance benchmarks to drive performance, often using a league table approach, so that those departments with the best performance are recognised as such and others are encouraged to make their way up the table.
- o As such, I think it is most effective where there are multiple business areas that are largely similar. Much of the early research looked at retail banking, and benchmarking branches with each other to drive performance.
- o Being completely honest, though, I have never seen Beyond Budgeting being used in practice. As an approach, I think many traditional organisations find it too radical. However, it works in some sectors, and if you are a start-up then there may be merit in looking into Beyond Budgeting in more detail.

YOUR NOTES FROM CHAPTER 7

Chapter 8

Top 10 Tips for Using Financial Ratios

In this chapter:

- Why do we use ratios?
- What are the top 10 ratios for most businesses?

So far, we have looked at the preparation and reporting of financial data, be that for historic performance or as part of a budget or forecast.

In this chapter we explore how to make effective use of the data that is available by using financial ratios.

It can be very difficult to compare the Income Statement, Balance Sheet and Cash Flow Statement of different companies, or even different business units with the same company. Often this is just a function of scale (it is difficult to compare the financial results and a very large company with a very small one) but also different industries have different financial structures, and this is reflected in the financial statements.

Using financial ratios is an effective way of addressing these limitations. It is also helpful to analyse performance from one year to the next and allowing trends to be identified.

The focus will be on ratios that can be calculated using externally published data (usually the financial statements). However, they can be applied to internal data to compare business units or to look at budget or forecast.

Context is everything with ratios, and they are most effectively used to stimulate questions about the financial performance of one entity compared with another.

The list is also, by necessity, a generic one, albeit based on ratios commonly used. Certain industries or companies may have an emphasis on some of these over others. It is important for you to understand which ratios are used most commonly in your company.

1   **Gross Margin**

- Gross margin is a measure of the profitability of the company, from the perspective how effective it is in producing goods or services.
- It looks at profit before administrative expenses are taken into consideration.
- It is calculated as follows:

$$\text{Gross Margin} = \frac{\text{Revenue} - \text{Cost of Goods Sold}}{\text{Revenue}} \times 100$$

- Gross margin is always expressed as a percentage.
- The higher the gross margin the better.
- Different industries have different gross margins, so it can be hard to make sensible comparisons between industries.
- However, it is an effective ratio for comparing companies within a given industry and identifying which is the most efficient.
- Gross margin should never be negative: that would mean the company is making a loss before overhead expenses, which would be a sure sign of impending doom.

2   Net Margin

- Net margin is like gross margin in that it is a measure of the profitability of the company.
- However, it looks at profitability after administrative expenses are taken into consideration, and so is a measure of how efficient the company is at turning revenue into profit.
- It is calculated as follows:

$$\text{Net Margin} = \frac{\text{Net Profit}}{\text{Revenue}} \times 100$$

- Net margin is always expressed as a percentage.
- The higher the net margin the better.
- Different industries have different net margins, so again it can be hard to make sensible comparisons between industries.
- However, it is an effective ratio for comparing companies within a given industry and identifying which is the most efficient.
- It is also effective at looking at performance over time: increasing net margins year on year are a sign that the company is becoming more efficient.
- Net margin can be negative if the company has made losses.

3   Earnings per Share (EPS)

- Earnings per share (EPS) is a measure of the profit attributable to the owners of the business, the shareholders.
- It expresses the profit made per share that is in issue.
- This does not mean that profit is distributed to the shareholders, although it could be in the form of dividends.
- It is calculated as follows:

$$EPS = \frac{\text{Net Income}}{\text{Number of Shares in Issue}}$$

- EPS is expressed as an absolute figure in units of currency (for example £1.15 per share).
- The higher the EPS the better.
- As with other Income Statement ratios, EPS is a useful measure to look at over time for a company.
- EPS is not particularly useful for comparing companies as they will likely have different numbers of shares in issue.
- You should also look out for new shares being issued to raise money (see Chapter 10) or as rewards to executives for performance. This will naturally reduce the EPS unless there is a corresponding increase in Net Income.
- There is also a similar measure called fully diluted EPS: This is the same calculation except that the denominator includes not just shares in issue but those that the company believes it will issue in the future. These are usually shares held for executives, as part of their remuneration, and which are expected to be issued soon.

4   Interest Cover Ratio

- This is a measure of the ability of a company to meet interest payments on debts out of its profits.
- It is calculated as follows:

$$\text{Interest Cover} = \frac{\text{Net Profit Before Tax \& Interest}}{\text{Interest}}$$

- Interest cover is expressed as an absolute value (for example 3.2 times).
- The higher the value the better: 3.2 times means that the company has more than 3 times the profits required to meet its interest payments.
- It is a measure of the resilience of a company to changes in its own profits or debt levels, and to external factors such as interest rates.
- If the level of interest cover is too low, then a small downturn in profits or increase in interest rates means it would not be able to pay interest on loans, which is frowned upon by those lending the company money.
- This is a ratio that can be used to compare companies in different industries as well as performance over time.
- There is a similar ratio for Dividend Cover which uses Net Profit as the numerator and Dividends as the denominator. However, dividends do not have to be paid (whereas interest must be paid) and so it is less useful overall as a ratio.

5   Price Earnings (P/E) Ratio

- This is a ratio that looks at the share price of a company relative to the profits that it has earned.
- It is commonly used by investors to determine whether a company is over- or under-valued.
- It is usually used for listed companies where the share price is known from the stock market.
- The calculation is as follows:

$$\text{Price Earnings} = \frac{\text{Share Price}}{\text{Earnings per Share (EPS)}}$$

- P/E ratio is always expressed as an absolute number.
- The share price is the current price at which the shares are being traded on the stock market.
- In general, a higher P/E ratio is better, although if too high then it might indicate that the company is valued too highly, and a share price reduction is to follow.
- Different industries tend to have different average P/E ratios, reflecting the market view as to how attractive that industry is.
- However, where a company has a lower P/E ratio than a competitor, it may indicate it is under-valued or that is has some problems.
- This ratio is also used as part of the evaluation when buying a company. In this case it is known as earnings multiple, and it uses the proposed price for the company as the numerator and earnings as the denominator.

6   Dividend Yield

- This is another investor-led ratio.
- It assesses the return that a shareholder gets from owning a part of a company, in the form of dividends.
- It is the equivalent of the interest rate you might expect to receive if you lent someone some money (which is effectively what shareholders do).

$$\text{Dividend Yield} = \frac{\text{Dividends Paid over 12 months}}{\text{Share Price}}$$

- Dividend yield is always expressed as a percentage.
- In general, the higher the dividend yield the better, although if it is too high, then investors might interpret the company as being too quick to return money to shareholders rather than continue to invest in the business.
- Some companies don't pay dividends at all, and so the ratio is redundant for them. Typically, start-up and technology companies have tended not to pay dividends. Instead look at Total Shareholder Return (see below).
- Dividend yields are often compared to the interest rate that could be achieved in, for example, a savings account.
- Dividend yields are expected to be higher than interest rates, as shareholders take a greater risk by investing in companies (they may go out of business with little chance of getting your money back) and dividends are not guaranteed. Therefore, in return, shareholders expect a higher return for their risk.

7   **Total Shareholder Return (TSR)**

- There are two reasons for investors to hold shares in a company:
    - To earn dividends on their shares (income)
    - To see the price of the shares go up over time (capital growth)
- Total shareholder return is a measure for investors to see how much they have gained overall by holding shares in the company.
- It is calculated as follows:

$$TSR = \frac{(\text{Current Share Price} - \text{Starting Share Price}) + \text{Dividends}}{\text{Starting Share Price}}$$

- TSR is usually expressed as a percentage.
- The Starting Share Price might be the purchase price of the shares (for an individual investor) but for the purposes of analysts it would be the share price at a certain point in time in the past.
- The Dividends should be those paid over the same time period as when the Starting Share Price was set.
- The higher the TSR the better and is likely to indicate a company performing well for its shareholders.

8   Current Ratio

- The current ratio is a measure of working capital, and the ability of the company to settle its short-terms debts, such as overdrafts with banks and amounts owed to suppliers.
- It is an indicator of cash flow strength.
- It is calculated as follows:

$$\text{Current Ratio} = \frac{\text{Current Assets}}{\text{Current Liabilities}}$$

- The current ratio is always expressed as an absolute figure.
- A ratio of 2 is generally considered desirable: this means there are twice the value of assets to meet the liabilities and is a healthy situation for the company
- A ratio of less than 1 suggests the company may have some difficulty in settling its debts in the short term and is an indicator of potential trouble.
- A ratio significantly above 2 can also be viewed as negative. It means that the company might not be efficiently managing its current assets, especially if a significant proportion of the current assets are inventory or debtors. See also the Working Capital Cycle in Chapter 6.

9   Debt to Equity Ratio

- Companies can finance their activities by borrowing money (debt) or by raising money form shareholders (equity).
- This ratio provides an indication of how the company has chosen to operate.
- It is calculated as follows:

$$\text{Debt to Equity} = \frac{\text{Total Debt}}{\text{Shareholders' Equity}}$$

- It is usually expressed as an absolute figure.
- As with other ratios, different industries typically have different debt to equity ratios.
- This is a ratio where it is not always easy to say whether higher or lower is better.
- Debt is not a bad thing, necessarily. It is usually cheaper as interest rates on loans are typically lower than dividends on shares, and interest payments are allowable for tax deductions whereas dividends are not.
- However, debt must be repaid, whereas shareholders do not necessarily. A very high debt to equity ratio might mean that the company cannot operate effectively as it must work to pay down the debt.
- There is a theoretical optimum Debt to Equity ratio. When I studied the theory, it was generally assumed to be 1.5, although this could vary significantly depending upon industry.
- Manufacturing companies tend to have higher ratios than service companies, as they must invest in factories and equipment.
- It is useful to compare companies in the same industry: a company with higher ratio might be viewed as a riskier business to work with.
- Also trends over time are important, and a rising ratio (along with some indicators form other ratios) might indicate a company facing debt issues.

10   Return on Capital Employed (ROCE)

- Return on Capital Employed (ROCE) is measure of profitability and how efficiently the company's assets are being used to generate profits.
- It is calculated as follows:

$$\text{ROCE} = \frac{\text{Earnings Before Interest \& Tax}}{\text{Total Assets} - \text{Current Liabilities}} \times 100$$

- ROCE is usually expressed as a percentage.
- The higher the ROCE the better.
- Different industries have different ROCE's, and so as with many of our other ratios, it is important to make comparisons with competitors in the same field.
- It is also a very useful measure of performance over time, and to assess if a company is becoming more, or less, efficient.
- In my experience, many companies set target returns for ROCE, especially when considering new investments.   Such new investments must exceed a target return to be considered favourably.

YOUR NOTES FROM CHAPTER 8

Chapter 9

Top 10 Tips for Shareholder and Investor Relations

In this chapter:

- How do external stakeholders make investment decisions?
- Where do they get their information from?
- What are they looking for?

We looked at stakeholders back in Chapter 1. This chapter looks at the external view that some of those stakeholders take of your company. We are particularly focusing on larger companies here with listed shares and bonds.

1   The External View

- For the purposes of this chapter will focus on the following stakeholders:
    - Shareholders: people and organisations that own part of your business.
    - Bondholders: people and organisations that have lent money to your business.
    - Banks: regulated organisations that provide deposit and loan facilities.
- This group of stakeholders have a common link: they provide the money that allows the company to operate, in both the short and long term.
- Without these stakeholders the company will not be able to survive.
- Whilst they are important stakeholders, they are often external to the company and therefore must make use of the information that is published.
    - There are exceptions to this: in an owner managed business, there are often a small number of shareholders who also run the business day to day
- Many of these stakeholders will make use of the ratio tools we looked at in the last chapter and will also using their own financial models to assess the future.

2   **Investor Relations: Who is Involved?**

- From the perspective of external parties, there are several people that might get involved:
    - Individuals: people who own shares or bonds in the company in their own name.
    - Buy-side analysts: these are people who usually work for large institutional investors that own a lot of shares or bonds. These are commonly pension funds, mutual funds or hedge funds. They are making decisions on whether a certain investment meets the stated strategy of the fund.
    - Sell-side analysts: these are people that usually work for brokers and make recommendations in respect of shares or bonds. These recommendations are commonly in the form of 'buy', 'hold' or 'sell' or similar words.
    - Corporate broker: corporate brokers are appointed by the company to act as the main interface with the stock market, assessing market conditions, the demand for your company's shares and actively marketing them to potential investors. They are similar in that regard to sell-side analysts but are 'cheerleaders' for the company itself and are not therefore taking a fully independent view. These brokers are sometime known as Nominated Advisers (Nomad).
    - Media: although the media to not have a formal investment in the company, their view of you and your results is an important consideration. They can be hugely influential, and there is frequently wide coverage of large or well-known businesses that people interact with regularly.
    - Corporate public relations advisors: these are also appointed by the company and provide advice on how communications should be made to external parties, in terms of form and content. Often get involved with dealing with the media.
    - Corporate lawyers: these are lawyers who are familiar with the requirements of being a listed company and will provide advice on disclosures that need to be made and their content.

129

- Corporate bankers: these are people who work for the banks, and who will take an interest in your performance, especially if you are borrowing money from them. They will also get involved in assessing whether to lend money to you in the future. They are assessing risks and rewards of any loans they have or make to the company.

- Recognising this is an extensive range of stakeholders, being able to manage these relationships is an important part of running a large company. Several company employees must therefore be engaged to support this. Different companies work in different ways, but here are some broad guidelines on who might get involved:

  - Chief Executive Officer (CEO): will have an important role in discussing company strategy and performance with external stakeholders.
  - Chief Financial Officer (CFO): will support the CEO in managing the relationships, with an emphasis on the financial performance and metrics.
  - Non-Executive Directors (including the Chair and Senior Independent Director): non-executive directors are representatives of the shareholders on the Board of the company. Their role is discussed in more detail in Chapter 11, but they are an important interface between the shareholders and the management team running the business day to day.
  - Investor Relations (IR): this may be an individual or a department, depending upon the size of the company usually. They prepare materials for investors that will be published and will also coordinate investor events and meetings. They are commonly the first point of contact for any shareholder or bondholder queries.
  - Treasury: as with IR this can be one or more people. They will primarily liaise with banks but will also be involved with bondholders and will be the primary point of contact for these.

- Corporate communications: many companies employ teams of people who generate internal and external communications. Part of their role is often to get involved with supporting publications aimed at shareholders and other investors, and they will also commonly be the first point of contact for any questions from the media.
- Company Secretary: this is a specific role required of larger companies. It is carried out by a suitably qualified specialist (sometimes a lawyer or accountant) and they are required to ensure that the company complies with all legal and regulatory reporting requirements. They will often liaise with other across the business to ensure that everything that needs to be disclosed is.
- Other specialists: companies may also get other people involved in their external stakeholder activities. This may include finance personnel (particularly those involved in preparing the published accounts), strategy or operational leaders.

3   How Does it Work?

- There is a rhythm to the way that engagement with stakeholders takes place.
- Companies have an annual reporting period, which commonly aligns with the calendar year (namely 31 December) although it does not have to, and many companies do have different year ends.
- Ahead of or close to the year end, a trading statement will be made which provides a brief update on performance for the year. This will contain little detail but will usually provide guidance relative to the expectations of the market.
- There will then be a period while the company completes its financial statements. For larger companies, this can take several months, although there are deadlines to be met (4 months for UK listed companies) and the generally acknowledged approach is the sooner you can publish the results the better.
- The company will set its own date to publish its detailed results. It is important that the company meets that date (see managing expectations below).

- The results will be published by a market statement, usually at around 7am, so that those that want to buy or sell shares have the information available to them before the markets formally open at 8am. The statement must be published in a prescribed way, so everyone who is interested can find it. Sometimes this is called a Regulatory News Service (RNS) statement.
- Later the same day, there is usually an analyst conference.
- A few days or weeks later, the annual report and accounts will be finalised and shared with shareholders. Historically this was a bulky paper document sent in the post, although these days it is more usually distributed through the company's own website to save cost.
- Later still there will be an Annual General Meeting (AGM) for shareholders.
- This process will typically take the company 4 -5 months to complete; a company with a 31 December year end will be looking to have all this done by the end of May.
- In the UK, listed companies must also report results at the mid-point of the year (known as interim results, or half year results) within 3 months of that mid-point date. The process contains some, but not all the elements of the full year results:
    - A brief trading update before or close to the half year date.
    - Market statement of the interim results, at 7am on the day set by the company.
    - Analyst conference to discuss the results and take questions.
- Interim results are briefer than the full year ones, and therefore contain less detail. They must still be prepared to the same standard, however, as any errors would be embarrassing to say the least.

4   Annual General Meeting (AGM)

- The AGM, as its name suggests is held once a year.
- There are rules around what notice must be given of the meeting, and how the agenda and resolutions are published. This ensures all shareholders are given an equal opportunity to attend.
- All shareholders, or their representatives, are entitled to attend.
- The meeting will be led by the Chair of the company

- There will usually be a discussion of the results, and an opportunity to raise questions of the Directors of the company.
- This will then be followed by several resolutions that shareholders are invited to vote on. These include:
  - Accepting the report and accounts;
  - The appointment of directors
  - The appointment of auditors;
  - The remuneration policy for senior executives of the company
- Often most of the votes on the resolutions are cast well in advance of the meeting, using a proxy voting system. I have seen over 95% of the votes being cast in this way, meaning that shareholders on the day have little influence on the outcome.
- Perhaps because of this, my experience is that few shareholders attend the meeting, unless there has been some particularly high-profile issue that they wish to discuss.
- Questions over the effectiveness of these meetings are not new.
  - John Brooks wrote about his experiences in the 1960s [12] although concluded there was value in at least allowing the CEO to show their personality largely in response to questions from the few small shareholders that turned up.
  - Regardless, they are requirement in company law and will continue to be a feature of the corporate calendar.

5   Analyst Conferences

- These are usually held twice a year, shortly after the year end and half year end.
- Attendance is by invitation. Usually, this will be recognised analysts (buy-side or sell-side) and may also include representatives of banks.
- There will be presentations of the results (usually led by the Chair, CEO and CFO) and an opportunity for the analysts to ask questions.
- Although a closed meeting, the information shared is considered public and so it should be assumed that anything said will be reported.

6   Other Events

- In addition to these cyclical activities, many companies also run other events for shareholders, analysts or potential investors to showcase the company and its activities.
- These are often called investor roadshows or capital markets' days.
- Sometimes this will involve investors visiting manufacturing sites or offices to get a greater understanding of the business, and to see the actual activities taking place.
- These are usually coordinated by the IR team, although others may be asked to get involved to demonstrate their area.
- There are also investor relation events where multiple companies and potential investors can meet in a semi-structured way. These are sometimes called 'speed-dating' events in that you have a set, limited, time to discuss the business with a potential investor or analyst. Usually each session is around 30 – 45 minutes and so the information shared must be brief.
- There may also be 1:1 meetings arranged with shareholders, analysts or investors. Care should always be taken to ensure that any information divulged in these meetings is the same as that in the public domain. If a particular shareholder is given significant information about the company that is not known by others, they could gain an unfair advantage when deciding what to do with their investment.

7   Managing Expectations

- A core aspect of all this investor relations activity is the managing of expectations
- Investors (or potential investors) will have expectations of your results.
- This is most obvious with the sell-side analysts, who support their buy/hold/sell recommendations with forecasts of performance and an assessment of how well the company has performed against these.
- However, all investors have some expectations and that is informing their decisions about whether, and how much, to invest in your company.
- These expectations are informed by several factors:
    - ○ Information published by the company, including historic results, strategic plans and market analysis

- o   Knowledge of the industry
- o   Knowledge of wider economic factors that may have an impact
- o   Experience of the analyst
- o   Guesswork!
- The company does not publish its own budgets or business plans as these are usually considered to be commercially sensitive and involve a fair degree of judgement.
- However, the company may give some public guidance as to the company's aspirations in the medium term.   Phrases such "looking to achieve double digit growth" or "improving profit margins" are ones I have seen used in this context, perhaps with a range of outcomes. For example, in 2016 Tesco plc publicly targeted a margin range of 3.5% - 4.0% by 2020 [13]
- Analysts use this information to generate their own forecasts. Where multiple analysts are looking at a company, their forecasts are averaged out, and the result is called the consensus forecast.

8   Events

- It is the nature of expectations that whilst sometimes these are met, often actual outcomes are better or worse than expected.
- Where it becomes clear through information available to the company (usually through monthly management accounts or forecasts) that the financial performance is going to be materially different to the market expectations (usually measured by the consensus forecast) then the company must publish that information.
- There is a bit of judgement here, as to what constitutes a material difference. The guidance is that this information that if disclosed, would have a significant effect on the price of the shares or bonds in issue [14].
  - o   This will vary from company to company, and most will take legal advice if they think there is a potential matter to be disclosed.
  - o   The disclosure of this information must be done swiftly, and usually though an RNS statement (as for results updates). This is to allow all investors to access the same information at the same time, so no one gains an advantage.

- o Commonly these announcements occur where a company is going to report an outcome lower than the market expectation. Hence, they have become known as profits warnings.
- o However, this does not have to be the case. If a company has won a significant new contract for example, then earnings may be enhanced materially, and this too would be worthy of disclosure.

9   Insiders

- Within any company there are a small number of people that have access to price sensitive information, as a matter of carrying out their roles.
- This is likely to include senior executives, those who prepare the financial results and forecasts and also advisers to the company who are required to know a lot of what is going on in order to provide suitable advice.
- These constitute insiders, and companies are obliged to maintain a list of these.
- Insiders are required to keep the information they know about the company confidential, as if the information were to be shared, someone might gain an advantage over other investors.
- Insiders are also restricted as to what they can do when it comes to buying or selling shares in the company.
- Often the timing of these restrictions is related to significant events for the company. These times are known as closed periods and include:
  - o Around the year end until the final results are published
  - o Around the half year end, until the results are published
  - o The period in the run up to the conclusion of a significant corporate event (for example buying a company or signing a large legal agreement).
- You should be advised if you are an insider, and if so when the closed periods are in operation.

10   Other RNS Statements

- Whilst we have focused on results announcements, there are other things that are commonly reported on through the RNS.
- These include:
  - Anyone that holds 5% or more of the shares in the company:
    - The company must report the names of those shareholders, how much they hold and any changes in shareholding once the 5% threshold is reached.
    - This allows other shareholders to know who the big (and potentially more influential) shareholders are.
  - Changes in Directors of the company (appointments or resignations).
  - Any other directorships that Directors in the company take with other companies, or that they resign from.
    - This allows shareholders to understand any links between the Directors and other companies that might influence their decision making.
  - Share acquisitions or disposals of Directors or Senior Executives.
    - The regulations state this must be done for all Persons Discharging Managerial Responsibilities (PDMR) which includes the Directors and anyone else that has access to inside information and can make decisions that affect the business [15].
  - The acquisition or disposal of a business or activity.
- Some of these are financial items, others are not. However, the key point is that, along with the financial information, these announcements are aimed at sharing a lot of the information an investor would need to make an informed decision.

YOUR NOTES FROM CHAPTER 9

Chapter 10

Top 10 Tips for Raising Money

In this chapter:

- Why do companies raise money?
- What options are there for raising money?
- What happens if a company runs out of money?

1   Raising Money

- At some point every company will need to raise money.
- If it is just starting up, then money will be needed to buy essential equipment or inventory to get things under way.
- Established businesses need money to expand or invest.
- Sometimes a business will need to raise money because something has gone wrong and without raising money the business will cease to exist.
- All debt needs to be disclosed in the published financial statements. It is essential for the external reader of the accounts to understand what the liabilities of the business are so they can have an informed view of its position.
- Debt will be classified into current (short-term) liabilities and long-term liabilities on the Balance Sheet and accompanying notes.

2   Types of Fundraising

- There are many factors to be taken into consideration when borrowing money.
- What is the money needed for?
  - Short-term requirements are generally better suited to short-term debts.
  - Long-term requirements to long-term debts.
  - Very long-term requirements by raising money from shareholders (new or existing).
- What is the current debt and equity position?
  - We saw in Chapter 8 that two of the ratios used by investors are the Debt to Equity Ratio and Interest Cover Ratio.
  - How these ratios look at a point in time, and how they would look after any financing, will have a significant influence on the approach a business takes to raising money.

- What wider factors might influence raising money?
    - There are certain phases in the economic cycle where it is easy to borrow money and others where it is harder.
    - Similarly, there are phases where raising money from shareholders is easier than others.
    - Sometimes these factors are applicable to all companies, at other times it might be related to specific market or sector.
- Regardless of how a company chooses to raise money, the financing activities will form part of the Cash Flow Statement.

3   Short-Term Debt

- As I have mentioned, short-term debt is best used for short-term purposes.
- A typical use is to fund working capital:
    - Where the cash coming into the business is less than that going out, but only due to the time is has taken to collect customer payments compared with settling supplier debts and building inventory.
    - We looked at working capital in Chapter 6.
- There are several ways to raise short-term debt.
- One way is to delay payment to suppliers:
    - In effect you are making your supplier give you an interest free loan.
    - I would advocate this being done only by agreement with the supplier.
    - Large companies have come under scrutiny for their payment practices where this has been imposed on their suppliers.
- Outside of this approach, the most common is to agree an overdraft facility with your bank.
    - As with a personal overdraft this allows you to spend more than you have with them, up to a pre-agreed limit.
    - The amount borrowed can be flexible and will likely vary day to day.
    - You will pay interest on the amount borrowed, usually at a relatively high rate.
    - The interest rate is usually variable and can be changed by the bank quickly.

- o Interest costs are an allowed expense for tax purposes, meaning you can reduce profits reported for tax by the amount of the interest.
- A further option is to use the amounts owed to you by your customers to raise money before they have paid:
  - o This would be done through a financial institution, who would advance you a proportion of the amount owed by your customers in advance.
  - o This is known as debt factoring or invoice discounting. The difference between the two is:
    - With Debt Factoring, the customer settles their invoice directly with the Factoring company, so customers are more likely to be aware of your factoring arrangement.
    - With Invoice Discounting, your customers still pay you directly; there is no need for them to know that a third party is involved.
  - o With either option you receive a proportion of the amount owed by your customers to you, the financial institution keeping the balance as a return on their loan to you.
- Overdrafts and advances on invoices tend to be relatively expensive ways of borrowing money.
- They are also usually repayable on demand (which is why they are classified as short-term loans) which means if the business does not keep up with repayments, the situation can quickly escalate.
- They are, however, very flexible and can allow the business to react quickly to cash flow demands.
- Provided the use of these facilities is genuinely for short-term reasons then they are a valuable and commonly used funding mechanism.

4   Long-Term Debt

- Long-term debt is very useful for funding activities that will benefit the business over a longer period.
- Examples are to buy new vehicles of computer equipment; items that will have a fairly long life.
- Banks and other financial institutions are a major source of long-term loans.

- o You will pay interest on the amount borrowed, usually at a lower rate than on an overdraft.
- o The interest rate may be fixed or variable.
- o Interest costs are an allowed expense for tax purposes, meaning you can reduce profits reported for tax by the amount of the interest.
- Often, the bank will require a charge over some or all the assets of the company.
  - o A charge is like a mortgage on your home: if you fail to repay the loans then the bank has rights over the assets and can sell them to repay their debt before anyone else.
  - o Charges on assets must be disclosed at Companies House, so that anyone dealing with the business knows that certain lenders have rights over the company.
- Another source of long-term debt is leasing. We looked at the accounting for leasing in Chapter 3.
  - o Leases are particularly useful for certain common assets such as vehicles or computer equipment, although almost any kind of physical asset can be leased.
  - o With a lease you pay a fixed monthly amount to use an asset, without owning it.
  - o Sometimes you are required to pay for the ongoing maintenance of the asset, although it can be included in the lease cost.
  - o The lease is usually for a fixed period, after which you can return the asset or pay to buy it from the leasing company.
- With long-term borrowing the assets are held on the Balance Sheet as assets, and the liabilities as long-term liabilities
  - o This is true of leased assets as well as those purchased directly with a loan.
  - o However, the liability (lease or loan) will usually be split between current and long-term, recognising that some of the loan will be paid within the next 12 months (current) with the balance falling due after that.
  - o The disclosure of this is an important aspect of financial accounting.

5   Corporate Bonds

- Corporate bonds are a specific form of long-term debt.
- They are made by issuing bonds to people and organisations outside the company.
- Bonds are usually issued in blocks of a fixed amount (for example £1,000), which is the par value, and for a set period.
- Bonds pay a regular return to those who own them. This is the same as interest but is known as a coupon for bonds
  - This may be fixed or variable but will be set out in the bond agreement.
  - The coupon cost is an allowed expense for tax purposes.
- Often (but not always) bonds are able to be traded on the open market
  - The market price of bonds is reflective of the view bondholders are taking of the performance of the company and its ability to repay the debt.
  - For example, if a bond with a par value of £1,000 is being sold for £600 then the view is likely to be that the company might struggle to repay the debt
    - Sometimes this is known as a junk bond (see below).
    - It does not mean the company won't repay the bonds, just that it has some work to do to convince bondholders it can, and to make sure it can.
  - Even if the market price of the bond changes, the amount the company pays in coupon, and the amount it repays at the end of the loan period does not
    - That generally means that nearer the end of the bond period the market price and the bond par value converge: why pay more for a bond than you will receive shortly?

6   Rating Agencies

- One of the sources of decision making for banks and bondholders are rating agencies.
- Some of the best known are Standard & Poor's (S&P), Moody's and Fitch Group.
- Each of these review the financial performance of the business and assess their ability to repay any debts: their credit worthiness.
- Each then assign a series of letters to the company's credit rating and these are commonly quoted in the financial press.
- These ratings are as follows. The ratings are from lowest risk to highest risk:

		Standard & Poor's	Fitch Group	Moody's
Investment Grade	The lowest risk:	AAA	AAA	Aaa
	• High probability of paying interest and the loan	AA	AA	Aa
		A	A	A
		BBB	BBB	Baa
	• Likely to be lower interest rates			
Speculative Grade /Junk Bond	The highest risk:	BB	BB	Ba
	• Some probability of default on the loan, or interest not being paid	CCC	CCC	B
		CC	CC	Caa
		C	C	Ca
		D	D	C
	• Likely to be higher interest rate for the lender			

145

- These ratings are usually only prepared for the largest companies.
- However, almost every company has a credit assessment made by one of the credit scoring companies
  - Dun & Bradstreet and Experian are two of the best known.
  - They provide a credit score and an indicative guide as to how much should be lent to the company, either by loan or through giving credit terms on invoices.
  - These are readily available to anyone, but you must subscribe to their service in order to access the information.
  - It can be a cost-effective way of understanding whether to trade with a company or provide a loan to them.

7   Private Equity and Venture Capital Funding

- Private equity funding is a way for a company to access funds from institutions.
  - The private equity holder buys some or all the shares of the company.
  - They become a significant shareholder.
- There is not the same commitment to pay interest as with other forms of borrowing.
- Those that invest in young businesses are often known as venture capital investors.
- The amounts can be significant, particularly relative to the size of the company.
- Private equity investors are often taking a significant risk on a company that may not have a proven track record of success.
- As such, they often base their investment on getting a significant return in the medium-term.
  - Commonly the medium-term is 3 – 5 years.
  - The return is usually generated through the sale of the shares to another private equity company of through an IPO (see below).
- Often private equity investors will play an active role in the operations of the company, sharing their expertise to the benefit of the business and their investment.

- Well known variations on the theme of private equity funding are:
  - Crowdfunding: where a company (usually a start-up business) raises money directly from small investors through an online platform.
  - The BBC's Dragons' Den: business owners pitch to a group of individuals and try to convince them to invest in their business in return for a shareholding, and business advice.

8   Shareholder Funding: Initial Public Offering

- Whilst all companies must have shares issued, they do not have to be made available for the general public to buy and sell.
  - Private companies do not have freely traded shares.
  - Public companies are those with freely traded shares.
- Many private companies do eventually decide that they want to raise a significant amount of money, and commonly they will do this by selling shares more widely than their existing shareholder base. This is known as an **Initial Public Offering (IPO)**.
- There are five common reasons for a company to pursue an IPO:
  - The company is major part of a larger group but is no longer seen as a core part of the business. The parent company wants to sell the smaller business and decides a stock market listing is most appropriate. I saw this when I worked for American Water in 2006/07.
  - Some of the investors in the company (which may be private equity or venture capital investors) want to realise some of their investment in cash.
  - The company wants raise funds for a significant investment or expansion. Sometimes this is linked to the acquisition of another business.
  - The company wishes to reduce its other debt (loans or bonds).
  - Privatisation of a state-owned company. In the UK at least there are fewer of these than there used to be following the privatisation activities of the 1980s and 1990s, but companies such as British Telecom and British Gas were privatised through IPOs.

- There are some common features of IPOs
  - The sums raised are usually huge (often several billions of pounds) and much larger than could be borrowed any other way.
  - This is generally done through having many individuals or organisations invest in the company.
  - IPOs are often underwritten by financial institutions, which means that if the shares fail to sell, the institution will buy them.
  - The company must publish a prospectus for the IPO. This will include information about the company, its financial performance and how it intends to use the funds generated.
  - The company will often get a lot of scrutiny in the run up to an IPO and afterwards. This can be challenging to a management team that may not be used to that.
  - Once the IPO has been completed the company will be listed on a stock exchange. This allows the shares to be easily bought and sold.
  - Common stock exchanges are:
    - London Stock Exchange (LSE) – UK
    - Alternative Investment Market (AIM) – UK
    - New York Stock Exchange (NYSE) – USA
    - National Association of Securities Dealers Automated Quotations (NASDAQ) – USA
    - Tokyo Stock Exchange – Japan
    - Hong Kong Stock Exchange – China
    - Shanghai Stock Exchange – China
    - Frankfurt Stock Exchange – Germany
- In return for their investment, shareholders will look for dividends and the price of their shares to increase.
  - Dividends are not an allowable expense for tax purposes.
- Once listed, a company will commonly be allocated to an index within the exchange.
  - This is us usually allocate don the basis of the company's size.
  - The company's size is determined by its market capitalisation.
  - Market capitalisation is calculated as the current price of the shares multiplied by the number of shares in issue.

- o For example, the LSE has the following indices:
    - FTSE100: the largest 100 companies
    - FTSE250: the next largest 250 companies
    - FTSE Small Cap: those companies not in the top 350 by size
    - FTSE All Share: all the companies on the stock exchange
- o Certain investment funds will use these indices to determine their investment strategy.
    - You may see a FTSE100 tracker fund, which will only hold shares in the top 100 companies as determined by the index.
- o Market capitalisation moves all the time, and so which index a company is in can be volatile.
    - Each index has a set point in time where it will reassess the constituents. Often this is quarterly.
    - Usually there are some parameters about 'promotion' or 'relegation' form one index to another, so it is not automatic. Those on the margins will be assessed by the index setter.
- o Which index a company is in can have an impact on the share price.
    - A company is in the FTSE100, for example, but its share price falls and therefore it has a lower market capitalisation.
    - As part of the review the company is relegated from the FTSE100.
    - FTSE100 tracking fund will have to sell their holdings in the company, which will probably further reduce the share price.
    - The opposite would be true of a company moved into the FTSE100.

9   **Shareholder Funding: Rights Issues**

- A company listed on the stock may seek to raise further funds from existing shareholders in the form of a rights issue.
- Some of the reasons for this are common to the reason for raising money in the first place through an IPO:
  - Pay down other borrowings
  - Major investment in the business for the future
- Since the shares are already listed, a great deal of information is already in the public domain. Nonetheless, shareholders will expect to receive more information about the company's plans to help them decide whether to invest or not.
- There is usually no obligation for shareholders to join a rights issue. However, if a shareholder does not take part then they will own less of the company than they used to, as a percentage ownership. This is known as dilution.
- In order to persuade shareholders to buy more shares, they must usually offer them at a significant discount to the current market price.
  - This has an impact on the overall price of shares in the market.
  - The expectation is that over time, the value of the shares will increase again as the company is successful.

10   **If it all goes wrong: Administration and Liquidation**

- Sometimes companies run out of money and cannot raise funds from any of the sources we have described in this chapter.
- The directors of the company are obliged to assess whether the company can settle its debts as they fall due.
  - If the company cannot then they must put it into some form of insolvency process.
  - Sometimes those that are owed money will force the company into an insolvency process.
- Occasionally these are high profile: as I was writing this book travel company Thomas Cook went into liquidation and retailer Bonmarché into administration.
- These are the two common forms of insolvency

- Administration involves the company acknowledging that is cannot currently settle its debts.
  - An administrator is appointed to run the company on behalf of the lenders.
  - The administrator will try to keep the business operating as normal.
  - Allows it time to negotiate with its lenders and potentially find some other sources of funding.
  - The administrators can sell assets to raise funds.
  - Sometimes private equity funds will buy companies in administration.
  - It is not necessarily the end of the company if funding or another buyer can be found (for example Wright Buses were bought out of administration).
  - It does create uncertainty for everyone that is a stakeholder of the company, particularly employees, suppliers and customers.
  - Lenders are likely to lose at least some of their money.
  - Shareholders will commonly lose all the money they have invested in the company.
  - There is usually some time pressure to resolve the cash shortfall in order to avoid liquidation.
  - A Company Voluntary Agreement (CVA) is a form of administration, where the company seeks to renegotiate its debts. These have become common in the retail sector, with the aim of renegotiating lease agreements with landlords and other supplier debts.
- Liquidation is a final step to closing the company:
  - A liquidator is appointed to sell as much of the company's assets as possible to raise funds for lenders.
  - Usually the liquidator recovers a fraction of the assets' previous worth, as it is a distressed sale which drives down prices.
  - Liquidation can follow on from administration, but not necessarily. For example, both Carillion and Thomas Cook went straight to liquidation.
  - Lenders are likely to lose a lot of their money
  - Liquidation usually means the shareholders lose all their investment and the company ceases to exist.

- o Some parts of the company might be saved, as part of the liquidation process. For example, Thomas Cook travel agent shops were bought from the liquidators by Hays Travel.
- Clearly every company wants to avoid this process. Hence the importance of cash management that we discussed earlier in this book.

YOUR NOTES FROM CHAPTER 10

Chapter 11

Top 10 Tips for Governance and Control

In this chapter:

- How do companies create governance structures?
- What are the roles of the PLC Board and Executive Board?
- How should risk be managed?
- What are the roles of internal and external auditors?
- What is changing in corporate governance?

Corporate governance is not limited to finance and it covers a range of legal, operational and disclosure matters as well as finance.

However, corporate governance is, in my view, about how the company raises, manages and spends money and therefore it seems appropriate to cover it in this book.

1   Corporate Structure

- All companies are required to have a board of directors.
- The board of directors have legal responsibilities for running the company, and are ultimately accountable to shareholders, regulators and the courts for their actions.
- For a larger, listed, company in the UK a common corporate structure is as follows:

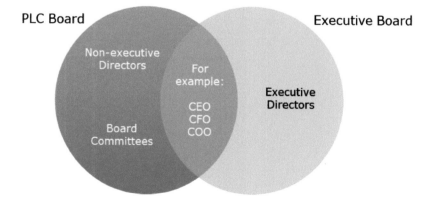

2   The PLC Board and Executive Board

- The PLC Board is the ultimate governance group of the company:
    - Typically made up of non-executive directors and executive directors.
    - Non-executive directors are not involved in the day to day running of the business and are there to represent shareholders and to challenge and guide the executive management.
    - The Chair of the company chairs this Board and is usually a non-executive director.
    - One of the non-executives is appointed as the Senior Independent Director (SID) and has a specific role to interface with shareholders about the performance of the Board and the Chair.
    - Executive directors are involved in the day to day running of the business. Typically, only two or three executive directors will be appointed the PLC Board, usually, but not always:
        - Chief Executive Officer
        - Chief Financial Officer
        - Chief Operating Officer
    - A listed PLC must have at least two independent non-executive directors.
    - The Company Secretary will attend the Board to take minutes and to ensure compliance with regulations.
- The executive directors will also be part of the Executive Board of the company.
    - The Executive Board (sometimes known as the management board) is a group of managers who have responsibility for the day to day running of the business and its activities.
    - The members will include functional and department leaders, depending upon the nature of the business and its chosen structure.
    - Executive board members who are not on the PLC Board will not be directors of the PLC.
    - They may, however, be directors of subsidiary companies.

- The terms of reference of the boards and responsibilities of the directors should be set out by the company as part of their annual report and accounts.

3   Committees

- Listed companies usually have at least three sub-committees of the PLC Board.
- The terms of reference for these committees should be made clear by the company though their annual report and accounts or on their website.
- Whilst each has delegated responsibilities, this is often in the form of carrying out activities and then making a recommendation to the full PLC Board.
- Audit Committee.
  - Typically has responsibility for overseeing the financial reporting of the business and the controls that are in place.
  - They will lead on the appointment of external auditors, making a recommendation to the PLC Board.
  - The internal audit function often reports directly to the audit committee.
  - The audit committee will usually review the report and accounts prior to recommending their acceptance to the PLC Board.
  - Is chaired by a non-executive director, typically one with a finance or audit background.
  - Usually other members of the finance department will be invited to present to the committee.
- Remuneration committee
  - Has responsibility for setting the pay for the Board and Executive Directors.
  - Usually guides on overall pay strategy for the company.
  - Must report on the remuneration paid to the members of the board and the basis of future remuneration though bonus and incentive plans.
  - Is chaired by a non-executive director.
  - Often a member of the human resources function will be invited to present to the committee.

- Nominations committee
  - o Has responsibility for all recruitment and appointments to the PLC Board, and usually the Executive Board.
  - o Commonly will oversee the talent development strategy for the company to ensure there is adequate succession planning in place.
  - o Is chaired by a non-executive director.

4 Being a Director

- Being a director is a significant commitment.
- There are obligations and duties set out in the Companies Act, and failure to adhere to these can have significant individual consequences.
- There are also increasing obligations from other legislation, particularly around health and safety and bribery, where directors must take steps to ensure compliance with the law or face the consequences.
- In company law there is no difference between a non-executive and executive director in this regard.
- I would always recommend that anyone thinking of becoming a director goes through some form of formal training as part of their appointment. The Institute of Directors' and Institute of Chartered Accountants in England & Wales are among the organisations that offer useful courses for aspiring directors.

5 Risk Management

- An important aspect of any corporate governance is the management of risk.
- The Institute of Internal Auditors (IIA) has an excellent guide to this area [16].
- The IIA highlight the role that the PLC Board plays in setting what is known as the risk appetite for the business: how much risk is the business prepared to take?
- As part of this the Board will identify the principal risks of the business.
  - o This is typically a list of 10 or so risks that have the highest priority.
  - o Priority is determined by combination of likelihood of the risk occurring and the impact on the company if it did.

- o Risks with a high probability and high impact are likely to be principal risks.
- o These risks must be disclosed in the annual report and accounts, and the actions being taken to manage and mitigate them explained.
- o It is likely that discussion of the risk will take place frequently at Board meetings throughout the year.
- The IIA sets out what an effective risk management framework should include, in order to ensure that everyone in the organisation is clear and aligned on the risks and how they are managed:

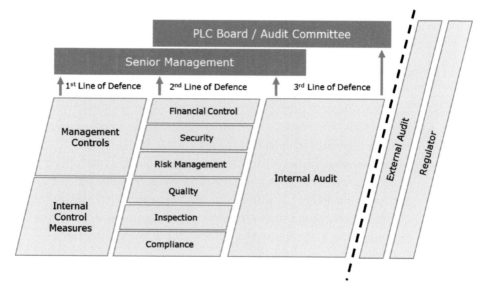

6   1st Line of Defence: Controls

- The operational management has ownership and responsibility for the risks in their area and implementing controls over them.
- This recognises that the best people to assess risks and the controls that are needed are often those carrying out the activities.
- It does require diligence on the part of the operational management, and an adherence to best practices and procedures.

- A common management control is segregation of duties:
  - This is where a person cannot initiate and authorise their own activities
  - For example, a purchase order is raised by one person, but the invoice is processed and paid by another
  - Another is where an expense claim is approved by someone other than the person claiming the expenses
- These control processes are designed to prevent any governance issues arising in the first place.

7   2nd Line of Defence: Quality Processes

- Quality processes are usually established by a centralised department (such as IT, finance, risk management or compliance) and set out the standards for common processes and facilitate the reporting of risks through the business.
- For example, the IT department will set standards on hardware and software, will control what can be used in the business and will mandate the frequency of computer password changes and so on.
- A common control process established centrally is the delegation of authority matrix that we discussed earlier:
  - This is a table that sets out for each major process what authority is required to proceed.
  - This is usually determined by type of activity and its size.
  - Some activities that are very high risk will be reserved for the PLC Board (for example acquiring another company) whereas routine transactions (such as raising a purchase order for materials) will be delegated down in the organisation.
  - It is important that you understand what your delegated authority limits are and that you adhere to them, as this is an important control process for many organisations.
- Another example are balance sheet reconciliations
  - These are usually carried out by the finance team, ideally monthly as part of the month end process.
  - The aim is to look at each of the accounts that form the balance sheet and agree those to supporting documents and evidence.

- o For example, the bank account reconciliation will compare the bank statements to the bank and cash records of the business, and make sure any differences can be explained and are understood.
- o The reconciliations are a valuable check to make sure that assets and liabilities are correctly recorded.

8   3rd Line of Defence: Internal Audit

- The internal **audit** function is an independent team of people whose role is to provide assurance to senior management (including the Audit Committee and PLC Board) through a risk-based approach to its programme of work.
- Internal audit functions often contain accountants, given the financial nature of many of the company's activities, but will also include experts form operational and commercial activities.
- The internal audit team will prioritise their work based on criteria and guidance agreed with the audit committee and will then visit company locations (and sometime those of supplier or customers) to review the operation of the 1st line and 2nd line controls. Their focus is very much control based.
- Good internal audit functions will not just carry out a series of checks for compliance but will also provide guidance on best practice, particularly around common activities carried out in other parts of the business, and how the team they are auditing can evolve to meet their and the wider organisation's objectives.
- It is important for the department to engage positively with the internal audit team
  - o They have a job to do, and their role is to protect and support the business.
  - o Internal audits rarely go any better if there is a confrontational approach taken by either the operational department or the internal audit team.
  - o No one expects perfection, and recommendations made should be in the spirit of making improvements and for the benefit of the business.

- Each internal audit should conclude with a report being prepared about the findings of the assignment team:
  - This should be discussed at a closing meeting with the manager of the department being audited.
  - There will likely be a series of recommendations, which will be prioritised, and implementation dates proposed.
  - It is essential for the department manager to make sure they understand and agree with the recommendations being made. They will be responsible for implementation, and too often I have seen recommendations made, and agreed to, that cannot then be implemented.
  - It is common for progress against internal audit recommendations to be monitored and reported to the audit committee. Failure to implement recommendations on time is a bad look.
- Generally internal audit teams are made up of employees of the company, supported by outside experts where necessary.
- Slightly confusingly, there is a market for outsourced internal audit functions, commonly provided by firms that are known for their external audit services.
  - There can be some cost savings to the company by making use of an outside firm.
  - Outside firms often come with access to wider expertise, potentially at the expense of depth of understanding of your business.
  - It is not permitted for the same organisation to provide internal and external audit services.
- Another aspect internal audit will get involved in is any so-called whistle-blowing complaints received by the company
  - These may be from employees or others.
  - Often refer to a breach of good practice by the company or its employees.
  - Are commonly anonymous.
  - Can be difficult to investigate.
  - The internal audit team will often lead an investigation, obtaining support from third parties where further expertise is necessary.

9   **External Audit**

- An external **audit** is a requirement for all large companies in the UK.
- In order to be an auditor, the firm must be registered with one of the regulatory bodies in the UK.
- The engagement is made by the PLC Board, with their work monitored by the Audit Committee.
- The appointment of new auditors used to be a rare occurrence. However, new regulations require:
  - The audit to be re-tendered at least every 10 years, although the incumbent auditor may be part of that process and be reappointed.
  - For the auditor to change at least every 20 years.
- The auditors' work is carried on behalf of the shareholders of the company.
- The external auditors should be completely independent of the company. To that end they should do little or no work on any other aspects of a business that they audit.
- Other stakeholders may use the assurance provided by their work to make decisions, but that is at their own risk. Case law is clear that the auditors do not owe a duty of care to anyone other than shareholders, unless separately engaged to do so.
- The audit process is geared around the main external reporting periods: the year end and half year end.
- Audit work is governed by auditing standards, and compliance with these is monitored by the regulatory bodies
- Much of the work is carried out just before and particularly after the year end.
- Before the year end the auditors might be familiarising themselves with the business, current issues, the control processes and any changes to systems or activities.
  - The external auditors cannot rely on the work of the internal auditors and must come to their own view on controls and processes.
  - Often system tests will be done at this stage, following transactions though all the processes to check they are working as they have been described.
  - Meetings with senior managers and finance personnel might be part of this phase.

- After the year end, the auditors will return and will perform more detailed reviews, now using the actual results for the prior year.
- The management team remain responsible for preparing the financial information and for making the judgements that are necessary to report the results.
- The auditors will review the critical judgements being made and check the main process to ensure the final results present a true and fair view of the business.
- The auditors will also review the non-financial sections of the annual report and accounts for consistency with what they know about the business and its performance.
- The conclusion is the independent auditor's report to the members of the company.
  - This used to be a one-page document but has expanded over the years.
  - It always appears just before the financial statements.
  - It will be signed by the statutory auditor, who is usually the senior partner of the audit assignment.
  - It sets out in some detail the work that has been performed, the approach taken and the audit firm's conclusion on key aspects of the business' performance in the year.
- As with the internal auditors, the external auditors have a job to do, and this generally goes better if you are open and transparent with them.

10   Current Topics on Governance

- Many aspects of this book are static
  - We talked in the first chapter about how the principles of accounting are hundreds of years old.
  - Many of the accounting standards were established years ago, although there are occasionally new standards or tweaks or existing ones.
- However, governance seems a lot more dynamic; there are frequently new requirements driven by legislation or stock exchange listing rules.
- Frequently these changes are a response to a corporate failing such as the Sarbanes Oxley Act, which was established in the US after Enron, WorldCom and other accounting scandals in the early 2000's.

- In the UK, the collapse of well-known companies such as Carillion and British Home Stores has triggered a review of the role of directors (particularly non-executive directors) and auditors.
- Furthermore, a Competition and Markets Authority review of the audit profession highlighted the dominance of the Big 4 firms (PricewaterhouseCoopers, KPMG, Deloitte and EY) and the impact of that on quality and price.
- Some of the implications of these reviews are still being established, but this much is clear at the time of writing:
  - There will be a new regulator for financial reporting, to be called the Audit, Reporting and Governance Authority (ARGA).
  - Auditors will have a duty of alert to report matters that concern them to ARGA.
  - Some action will be taken to make the audit market more competitive and allowing smaller firms to bid for work (possibly as joint auditors with larger firms).
  - There will be greater separation of audit and non-audit activities of the audit firms (particularly the Big 4).
  - There are likely to be strengthened legal duties for Directors.

YOUR NOTES FROM CHAPTER 11

Summary

I hope that you will have found this book of real benefit.

As I said in my introduction, the aim was to help you understand the language of finance. You may not be fluent, yet, but I hope that you are able to have deeper and more effective conversations with your finance colleagues.

In terms of actions you can take, I would recommend:

- That you build connections with your finance colleagues.
- Get to understand how the finances work for your business.
- Ask which key ratios or performance measures are used.
- Share your business knowledge with the finance team.
- Remember the key questions that you can ask:
  o   What has happened?
  o   What assumptions have been made?
  o   What does this mean for the business going forwards?
- If you have enjoyed it, recommend this book to your colleagues!

Thank you for reading.

Matthew Harris

Other books in the series and contact details can be found at
www.100toptips.com

Glossary of Terms

Accounting period: the time period (month, 3 months, 6 months or year) for which the accounts have been prepared.

Accounting policies: a summary of the choices a company has made in how to account for items, where there is a choice of approach permitted by **accounting standards**.

Accounting standards: the rules and guidance as to how items should be recorded in the financial statements.

Accrual: an accounting entry made for costs incurred but where the invoice has not yet been received.

Accruals accounting: the process of matching accounting for transactions to the period that they occurred, not necessarily when they were paid for.

Amortisation: an accounting entry that recognises that **intangible assets** have a finite life and therefore are worth less over time as they are used.

Assets: items held for use in the business, and which are expected to allow the business to generate income and cash in the future.

Audit: a review of the financial processes, controls and statements. Can be an internal or external audit.

Balance Sheet (also known as Statement of Financial Position): one of the primary financial statements showing the assets and liabilities of the business at a point in time.

Bank loans and overdrafts: money borrowed from a financial institution and shown on the balance sheet as a **liability**.

Budget: a financial plan for the year ahead.

Capital allowances: a concept used in **tax accounts** to reflect the usage of an asset over time. Like depreciation but with legally defined rates.

Capital expenditure (capex): payments to acquire or improve **assets** that will be used in the business for more than 12 months.

Cash Flow Statement: one of the primary financial statements showing the sources and use of cash of the business over a period.

Chart of accounts: the list of codes that shows **cost centres** and account headings that allow the business to record, report and analyse its financial performance.

Corporation tax: money that must be paid to the tax authorities, based on profits for the company, but with adjustments for items such as **capital allowances**.

Cost centre: a section of the **chart of accounts** that denotes a part of the business.

Cost of goods sold: the costs incurred by the business in manufacturing of goods or supplying services.

Credit: one half of double-entry bookkeeping that records liabilities and income.

Credit control: the process of managing the amounts owed by customers. Part of managing **working capital**.

Creditors: see **Payables**.

Consolidated accounts: the set of accounts for large group with multiple subsidiaries, which represents the entirety of the financial performance of the group.

Cost of capital: the cost that the business incurs in financing its activities, expressed as percentage.

Current assets: assets of the business that are likely to be converted into cash within the next 12 months. Includes **inventories**, **receivables** and cash.

Current liabilities: amount owed by the business and which are due to be repaid within the next 12 months. Includes **accruals**, **payables**, overdrafts and often **provisions**.

Debit: one half of double-entry bookkeeping that records assets and expenditure.

Debtors: see **Receivables**.

Delegation of authority matrix: a list of the limits that an individual can spend, usually categorised by type of spend and amounts of spend.

Depreciation: an accounting entry that recognises that **fixed assets** have a finite life and therefore are worth less over time as they are used.

Discounted cash flow: the future cash flow of an assessment reduced to reflect the time value of money.

Dividends: amounts paid to shareholders out of retained **reserves**.

Double-entry bookkeeping: the basic building blocks of accounting. All transactions are recorded as **debits** or **credits**.

Earnings before interest, tax, depreciation and amortisation (EBITDA): a measure of profit that excludes depreciation and amortisation.

Earnings before interest and tax (EBIT): profit after all operating and other income or expenses are taken into consideration, but before interest income/expense or corporation tax.

Earnings before tax (EBT): profit after all operating and other income or expenses and interest are taken into consideration, but before corporation tax.

Equity: the portion of a business owned by shareholders. Includes share capital and reserves.

Financial statements: the published summaries of the financial performance of the business.

Fixed assets: physical assets acquired for use in the business, that are expected to have a life of at least 12 months. Sometimes called tangible fixed assets.

Fixed asset register: a list of all the fixed assets held by the business.

Forecast: a projection of the company's financial results, usually to the end of the current financial year.

General ledger: the principal accounting record that includes and summarises all accounting entries.

Generally accepted accounting principles (GAAP): the collection of legislation and **accounting standards** regulations that govern the preparation and presentation of accounts.

Goods receipt note (GRN): a document that confirms the condition and quantity of goods or services received.

Gross profit: the profit achieved by the business from producing goods or delivering services, before any administrative expenses are taken into consideration.

Impairment test: a comparison of the market value of a long-term asset with its net book value. If the current market value is less, then the net book value must be reduced to match.

Income Statement, also known as the Profit & Loss Account: one of the primary financial statements showing income and expenditure for a period.

Initial Public Offering (IPO): sale of shares to the public, which will then be traded on a stock exchange.

Intangible assets: **non-current assets** of the business that cannot be physically seen. Examples are goodwill and patents.

Internal rate of return: an **investment appraisal** technique that looks at the discounted cash flow associated with a proposed investment and compares that to **cost of capital** for the business.

Inventory: the stock of raw materials, work in progress that will be made into products, and finished goods that are available for sale.

Investment appraisal: techniques used by the business to determine whether (or which) long-term investment plans should go ahead. **Includes payback period, net present value** and **internal rate of return**.

Liabilities: obligations that the business must pay someone in the future.

Leases: a form of financing whereby a company makes use of a fixed asset in return for a payment to a finance company.

Management Accounts: a summary of the financial performance of the business for use primarily by employees. Usually produced monthly.

Net book value (NBV): the current value of a long-term asset after accounting for depreciation or amortisation.

Net present value (NPV): an **investment appraisal** technique that looks at the discounted cash flow associated with a proposed investment and compares that to the initial cost.

Non-current assets: all assets that are expected to be used in the business for at least 12 months. Includes **fixed assets** and **intangible assets**.

Non-current liabilities: amounts owed that are not due to be repaid for at least 12 months. Also known as Long Term Liabilities.

Operating expenses (opex): the costs of running the business which are incurred regardless of the activity.

Operating profit: the profit for the business after taking into consideration the operating expenses.

Payables (also known as Creditors): amounts due to suppliers for goods and services supplied by them and which have been invoiced.

Payback period: an **investment appraisal** technique that looks at how quickly the amount spent on an investment will be recovered.

Prepayments: an accounting entry made where goods or services have been paid for but will be used over future periods.

Provisions: an accounting entry made for costs likely to be incurred, but where the exact amount or timing are uncertain.

Purchase order (PO): a document that confirms the intention to buy goods or services from a specific supplier.

Receivables (also known as Debtors): amounts due from customers for goods and services supplied to them.

Residual value: the estimate value of a **fixed asset** when it is expected to be sold by the business.

Requisition: the initial request from someone in the company to acquire some goods or services.

Reserves: an accumulation of all the net profits of the business since its inception, less any dividends paid out.

Revenue recognition: the accounting rules for recording the sales made by the company, governed by IFRS15.

Share capital: the money originally paid by shareholders to fund the company.

Shareholder: an individual or organisation that owns part of a business.

Statement of Financial Position: see **Balance Sheet**.

Statutory accounts: the financial reports required to be produced and published by law and regulation.

Tax accounts: accounts produced for the purpose of calculating the corporation tax liability for the company.

Trial balance: a summary of the **general ledger** used to show that the debits equal the credits.

Useful economic life: the number of years that a **fixed asset** is expected to be used in the business before being retired or sold.

Work in progress: goods that are partially assembled, or services that have been partially delivered to customers.

Working capital: the money required to keep the business operating on a day to day basis. Includes **inventories** and **receivables** less any **payables** and **accruals**.

References

I have made use investopedia.com in many of the definitions used throughout this book.

[1] See article by James Pickford in the Financial Times on 14 February 2019

[2] See Christies (https://www.christies.com/summa-de-arithmetica-the-28300.aspx?saletitle=)

[3] See article on What is GAAP? (https://corporatefinanceinstitute.com/resources/knowledge/accounting/gaap/)

[4] See UK Accounting Regulation: An Historical Perspective by Robert G Day (http://eprints.bournemouth.ac.uk/3074/1/296.pdf)

[5] There are many articles by Deloitte on this subject. A good introduction to their thinking is here: https://www2.deloitte.com/content/dam/Deloitte/us/Documents/finance/us-fas-cfos-play-four-critical-roles.pdf

[6] See Stuart Leung (https://www.forbes.com/sites/salesforce/2014/09/13/sorry-spreadsheet-errors/#7d06464656ab)

[7] See Christiane Soto (https://blogs.oracle.com/smb/10-of-the-costliest-spreadsheet-boo-boos-in-history)

[8] The Chartered Governance Institute (https://www.icsa.org.uk/assets/files/free-guidance-notes/contents-list-for-the-annual-report-of-a-uk-company.pdf)

[9] *The Great Game of Business* by Jack Stack and Bo Burlingham

[10] See https://kissflow.com/procurement-process/guide-to-procure-to-pay-process/

[11] See the Beyond Budgeting Roundtable www.bbrt.org

[12] *Business Adventures* by John Brooks, Chapter 10: Stockholder Season

[13] See FT.com (https://www.ft.com/content/96ffafc6-ac19-3134-ba77-983f4e728ea9)

[14] Financial Conduct Authority, Disclosure and Transparency Rules 2.2

[15] See Thomson Reuters Practical Law (uk.practicallaw.thomsonreuters.com)

[16] https://www.iia.org.uk/resources/audit-committees/governance-of-risk-three-lines-of-defence/

Index

About the Author

Matthew Harris BSc FCA

Matthew is a qualified chartered accountant (FCA) with over 20 years of financial and management experience with engineering and manufacturing companies in the UK and the US. After graduating from the University of Warwick, Matthew qualified as an accountant with Price Waterhouse.

After qualification, Matthew moved into industry, joining the finance team of BMW (UK), where he was responsible for financial accounting, the finance systems and managing the budgeting and reporting processes.

Matthew moved to Thames Water, where he led the integration of business planning activities across the global organisation, before moving to American Water, where he led the integration of their business reporting in 2005 and the subsequent Initial Public Offering process in 2006 and 2007.

Over the last 10 years, Matthew has led Divisional Finance teams in Hanson UK and Costain Group, driving the transformation of the finance functions in those organisations.

Most recently, Matthew was Group Strategy & Risk Director for Costain Group, leading the development of group strategy and linking that to the principal risks of the business.

Matthew was training manager for Price Waterhouse, Windsor, and has taken his passion for learning into his later roles. Matthew was also a founder member of the learning and development board of Costain, shaping the training strategy for the company.

In 2018, Matthew established his own training and development business, and now works to assist organisations make their finance functions more strategic, customer-focused and supportive of broader corporate activities. He also helps the wider business understand business finance and appreciate the role a modern finance function can play in supporting growth. He leads finance for non-finance workshops, business partnering programmes and strategy training sessions for clients. He is also an executive and team coach.

Matthew has also been a guest lecturer at the University of Warwick Business School and is an associate facilitator for the strategy programmes of the ICAEW.

In 2017, Matthew was named a Director of the Year by the Institute of Directors, London & South East Region, in recognition of his leadership and contribution to people development in a large and complex organisation.

Matthew is an alumnus of the Executive Development Program of the Wharton School of the University of Pennsylvania, the Deloitte CFO Development Programme, the PwC Leaders Development Programme and IMD Strategic Finance course.

Matthew is also a Non-Executive Director of Autistica, the UK's leading autism research charity. Autistica harness the potential of cutting-edge science to improve the lives of everyone affected by autism by funding and promoting ground-breaking medical research, improving understanding of autism and advancing new therapies and interventions. The vision is a long, healthy, happy life for autistic people and their families.

Acknowledgements

Whilst this is by no means an autobiography, it does represent the distillation of thoughts gathered through my entire working life. As such, it seems fitting to recognise those who have contributed to this book, even if indirectly. I have, of course, made every effort to make the contents accurate and any errors or omissions are mine.

Most importantly, I am grateful to my wife, Philippa and son, Jake, for their enduring support and patience. Throughout my career, my working hours have often been long, and consequently my presence at home unpredictable, but they have been a constant source of strength.

The early part of my career was shaped by some great finance leaders who generously offered inspiration, support and leadership at important times. Sandra Kelly, Alasdair Marnoch, Chris Bunker and Ellen Wolf have each shared their experiences with me and I almost certainly underappreciated their contribution to my success at the time.

I have, of course, worked with a great many other people throughout my career. There are far too many to name, but I have been genuinely grateful for the backing and guidance of those around me. I have always had the view that success is a team effort, and to the extent that I have had success, I recognise it was only possible because of the support of others.

Some of those colleagues have also become great friends, and I have continued to enjoy their wisdom, reflections and company long after we have stopped working together: Kathi Hambleton, Paul Pavey, Richard Tremellen, Catherine Wilcox, Julie Parmenter, Paul Milne, Pauline Clovey, Sarah Hunt, Rob Bloor, Allan Koodray, Marianne Taylor, George Patrick, Mark Atkinson, John Paterson, Fiona Hornby, Karim Jaffer, Jenny Tomkins, Mandy Swallow and Shafali Shown-Keen have all been hugely influential and supportive to me.

More recently, I have been establishing my own business activities. This has been a new challenge, and I am thankful for the guidance of Jerry Brown and Dave Buffham as I set out on this journey. I am grateful to the ICAEW Academy, who gave me my first contract for work. I want to particularly recognise the support I have had from Mike Pilkington and Paula Oliver in helping me grow in confidence in these early stages.

Ian Munro was the inspiration behind the book, and I appreciate his enthusiasm and encouragement, even as I missed my self-imposed deadlines! Nick Marlow, John Peters, Lisa Weaver, David Roden and Chet Oktay have also given me the benefit of their experience as I moved from the corporate world.

Finally, I would like to say thanks to Nicky. We only met as I started to write this book, but she helped me go through my archive and to put my thoughts into order and context. Without her advice, the finished product might have been very different.

Matthew Harris

November 2019

BV - #0037 - 161219 - C0 - 234/156/10 - PB - 9780993465895